The Pick-and-Screen Offense
for Winning Basketball

THE PICK-AND-SCREEN OFFENSE FOR WINNING BASKETBALL

Len Horyza

Parker Publishing Company, Inc.
West Nyack, New York

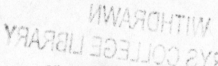

Library of Congress Cataloging in Publication Data

Horyza, Len.
    The pick-and-screen offense for winning basketball.

    Includes index.
    1. Basketball—Offense. 2. Basketball—Coaching.
I. Title.
GV889.H67   1984   796.32'32   83-26346

ISBN 0-13-676131-3

Printed in the United States of America

Dedication

In memory of my long-time friend and assistant coach, Harvey Buron, whose dedication to fundamentals helped build our program. His loyalty and friendship will always be remembered.

More importantly, Coach Buron was an inspiration to all the players and coaches he came in contact with.

FOREWORDS

I have followed prep basketball for over 40 years and never have I seen better prepared young performers than those on Len Horyza's Cretin squads—loaded with confidence, and equipped with sound fundamentals and techniques.

Horyza has a way of putting a coat of polish on raw material as quickly as any coach I have ever followed. His teams excel at the picks and screens that are so essential to the balanced attack. Even with young, untested material, it is soon evident that Horyza's teams play with a soundness that exudes coaching skills.

This book should be an enormous help to coaches seeking an improved offense. Horyza knows the game of basketball as few do. More important, he has the knack of implanting his knowledge in young minds and bodies. Horyza's methods, in short, are winning methods.

Don Riley
Columnist
St. Paul Pioneer Press

The one phrase heard constantly when a sports writer interviews a basketball coach about to play Cretin High School is, "We are going to have to beat them; they won't beat themselves."

Sometimes the obvious next line goes unspoken, but more often than not the opposing coach will look the sports writer in the eye and say, "Len Horyza is a tremendous coach."

Players, fans, and sports writers have realized for 19 years that Len Horyza is, indeed, a tremendous coach.

It makes no difference if Cretin has good personnel or mediocre personnel. The Raiders are going to battle for 32 minutes or more. They are going to pester the dickens out of the opponent defensively. When the Raiders have the ball, they are going to run a disciplined, controlled, opportunistic offense. They are always going to work until they get the best shot available to them.

No high school team in the metropolitan Twin Cities area is more effective at sharing the ball than Cretin. Patience and unselfishness are bywords of Horyza-coached teams.

Playing defense against the Raiders must, to even a strong opponent, seem as if one is attempting to eat soup with a fork. No matter how many of Cretin's options you stop, countless more are going to filter through your defense. The foe gets tired playing defense and Horyza's team is still probing for the best shot—all the while, of course, picking and screening the defense into submission.

Another coach in the St. Paul City Conference once told me, "When I have a championship contender, there is no one I would less like to play against than Len and his club."

Cretin, to be sure, has a giant-killer reputation.

After a pause to reflect, however, that same coach said, "Of course, if Len has better material than I do, that's when he's really murder to face. Can you imagine all that disciplined strategy coming at you . . . and being out-horsed on top of it?"

Horyza lives, sleeps, eats, breathes basketball. Among his many off-season connections with the sport has been as clinician at a popular summer basketball camp at St. John's University in Collegeville, Minnesota.

"Len is a great addition to our staff," said St. John's coach Jim Smith. "His method of teaching the game to the kids is phenomenal. He knows basketball inside out, but what really comes through to the kids is his love for the game. The kids see that and relate to it. Len's dedication adds meaning for youngsters."

No wonder, then, that Cretin basketball grads are known for their fundamental soundness when they get to college.

Last winter, many of Horyza's former players tossed an impromptu fiftieth birthday party for their former mentor. The feeling was unanimous that Horyza's disciplined approach had served these players well in later years, both on and off the basketball court.

Perhaps Horyza's most famous ex-player is Paul Molitor, the great Milwaukee Brewer third baseman. Len once told me that Molitor applied a better one-man press on Cretin opponents than any multiple-player press the coach ever devised.

Molitor returns the compliment. "I've been privileged to play for many great coaches in my athletic career," he said. "Len Horyza ranks with any of them. He's knowledgeable and he's good at explaining why certain things work and others don't. He commands respect."

Respect.

That says it all about the man . . . and his teams.

Mike Augustin
Sports Writer
St. Paul Dispatch—Pioneer Press

THE ADVANTAGES OF THE PICK-AND-SCREEN SYSTEM

This book is for the coach who likes to share ideas. I'm hoping it raises questions that some coach can answer or want answered. A coach might have the exciting conclusion or alternative to a certain play we are using. I don't know everything about basketball, but I do know that this system will bring about the discipline that all coaches would like to have.

This offense will be adaptable to your way of thinking and your offensive patterns, whatever they may be. The strongest selling point of this system is that it develops a pride in shooting, rebounding, and even movement without the ball.

This offense has worked for me for 19 years. It is one offense that works no matter what material you have; and the better the material, the better the results.

Although this offense is a patterned one, its options are unlimited, and therefore, very difficult to stop. This system has another advantage: When the season starts you are ready to coach, because you don't have to change anything—just polish what you have. Many coaches have to change their system each year to fit their personnel; *this* system doesn't demand great quickness, speed, or jumping ability. It just needs an aggressive player who wants to win.

Every offense has a certain play for special situations. Imagine having a special set of players every time you come down the court. With this system you have a choice of special plays every time you have the ball.

With the disciplined Pick-and-Screen system, you know exactly what your players are going to do; you have complete control.

The Pick-and-Screen offense is not a slowdown offense. The players are always looking for the shot, but not until the entire team is set the way you want them to be. The beautiful thing about this offense is the way one play blends into another. Your team is on the move all the time. Opponents will think you are running "The Passing Game."

In the Pick-and-Screen offense, you are coaching toward four offensive goals:

1. Picking to shoot a good percentage shot. This helps the players who can't score on their own.
2. Making sure each player knows what's going on at all times. This gives each player a set of standards by which to evaluate himself and his teammates.
3. Working for area rebounding position. This eliminates any chance rebounds.
4. Controlling your opponents' defense by forcing them out of their usual movement patterns. In this manner you can control the tempo of the game.

This offense is run without verbal keys. The offense is initiated by movements of the guards and center. In every set of the Pick-and-Screen offense, the guards determine the set plays by the way they pass and where they cut. The center determines which set you are in by his position on the floor. This method allows the players without the ball to be always moving with *purpose*. This coaching point also allows each player to have the best possible rebounding position.

THE ADVANTAGES OF THE PICK-AND-SCREEN OFFENSE

The Pick-and-Screen offense allows your players to consistently free themselves to shoot their highest percentage shots. In this offense there are so many options that the opponents cannot prepare a defense to stop it. Even if teams scout you and know every move that you will make, your players will take pride in picking apart these defenses.

The Pick-and-Screen tears apart pressure defenses by forcing them to switch, which creates a "fish," meaning a mismatch. Your team becomes the taller team during the course of the game; each of your players grows three to four inches.

The Pick-and-Screen offense keeps the opponent's defense from sagging and giving weakside help. It forces the defense to stay balanced so that they cannot double up on any one player.

With the Pick-and-Screen you can bring the opponent's big man up front or their small man deep, where they are not coached to play. This causes a confusion in the defensive play of your opponents which allows you to score some easy baskets.

The Pick-and-Screen *always* gives your team excellent rebounding positions. You will be introduced to the "Big Three" in rebounding. By using the "Big Three" method of rebounding, along with some basic rules for the guards and deep men, your team can improve their offensive rebounding efficiency by 30 percent or *more*. Because rebounding is so important to this offense, an entire chapter (Chapter 8) is dedicated to it.

Each player knows what the next player is doing at all times. Statistics show that at least 60 percent of all points scored are tip-ins, steals, free lance baskets, and free throws. But what about the other 40 percent? With this system, you and (more importantly) your players know exactly what is happening during the times you are setting up these 40 percent chances of your total offense. This cuts down on a coach's frustration caused by players doing their "own thing." It is said that free-lance ball players have more success against pressure than controlled-set offensive players have. It is also said that controlled-type players have more success against zones. In this system, a coach can take the free-lance player and make his moves the initial steps in the development of a controlled offense. In this manner, you will develop a complete offensive ball player.

The Pick-and-Screen offense can be used on every level of coaching. It is simple enough for young players to master and sophisticated enough for college teams. With this system you can start a successful new program or substantially improve an old one.

The Pick-and-Screen gives everyone on the team something to do on every set play. It sets the stage for the discipline needed in every phase of the game.

Coaches interested in improving the discipline of their team will profit by studying a basketball offense founded on statistical data. This offense was put together piece-by-piece from this data, and it has become a synchronized scoring machine.

Almost all coaches teach good sound offensive fundamentals, but very few coaches have put together a controlled offense initiated by the fundamentals they teach. However, this can be accomplished by the Pick-and-Screen system.

Because of the effectiveness of this system, your opponents will try desperately to beat you by employing zones and a variety of pressure defenses.

This book will show various cutting and screening patterns to successfully attack every kind of zone and pressure defenses. It will also show the Pick-and-Screen in the transition game, and in out-of-bounds situations. In other words, this is an entire playbook on the Pick-and-Screen system.

Every coach wants to win. Pick-and-Screen basketball means winning basketball.

Acknowledgments

I would like to express my sincere gratitude to all my fine players over the years who made our disciplined basketball part of their lives; to my wife Betty and my children for sharing and being part of the team; to my mother, who always encouraged me to work hard.

I also want to thank Bill Stewart, my freshman coach for several years; my daughter and typist Mary (Horyza) Miller; my proofreaders Don Geng, John Hughes, Rob Peick, and John Walsh; my present and past assistant coaches and managers; and Cretin High School, for having confidence in my coaching ability. To all of you, I give my sincere thanks.

TABLE OF CONTENTS

1

THE PICK-AND-SCREEN THEORY

WHY THE PICK-AND-SCREEN?

In the early years, I watched a lot of major college games and kept statistics on:

1. Where most of the shots were taken from.
2. What type of shots seemed to be the best percentage shots.
3. How players freed themselves for their shots.
4. How many bad shots were taken.
5. Where most of the rebounds came off the boards.
6. Which team got the most rebounds—and why.

I also attended high school and small college games with these same statistics in mind. Although I had had previous ideas, even as a player, I used this information to help substantiate my own thoughts on basketball. This system was built on the positive data that was gathered while trying to eliminate all the negative data.

The Pick-and-Screen philosophy, techniques, and fundamentals are largely based upon this statistical data.

The first year we used this system ended up a winning season, but we still felt we were limited in our offensive attack.

When we watched other teams play or attended clinics, we looked or listened for ideas that could possibly be used in this system. We never listened with the idea of using any other system. We knew what we wanted to accomplish—we wanted to free shooters for their best possible shots, to get balanced scoring from our players, and to be able to handle all types of defenses while controlling the offensive boards. It's a lot easier to add a certain move to your system than it is to put in a whole new system.

We started to piece together an offense that we now call the Pick-and-Screen system. Our players seem taller to us now. In fact, even a poor player has a chance to compete because of the effectiveness of this offense.

DEFINITION OF SCREEN

The first step to this system is to define what is meant by a *screen*. We define it to our players as "the legal action by a player who, without causing contact, delays or prevents an opponent from reaching a desired position."

This rule book definition is the basis of this system. The key words are *delay* or *prevent*. The players must understand that if they are playing against a well-coached team, they are not going to screen and pick perfectly all the time. All they are asked to do is screen-and-pick to delay the defense so that the offense can take their best percentage shots.

Every player screens a little differently. However, they should not move once they are set. This coaching point is a must. The screener should not brace himself for the charge. The screener is not allowed to put his arms out in front of him. We tell our players that if they cushion themselves for the charge, they will be called for a foul. The feet of the screener should be spread a little wider than shoulder width to take up more room on the court. His knees should be slightly bent. His arms should hang loose at his sides, with his back in a straight position, rather than bent over. If a defender bumps the screener, we want contact through the chest area. This is the way we teach our players to take the charge (offensive or defensive).

The screener should not fake a tough charge by falling down if it can be avoided, because he is no good to this offense if he is on the floor.

Most coaches think the screen is a very basic fundamental and is taught by every coach. Our data proves otherwise. As basic as the screen might be, you will find players falling down, bracing themselves, and moving after they are set. The fundamentals of the screen must be drilled constantly if you want to be a good screening team.

DEFINITION OF PICK

A pick is an offensive player's manipulation of a defensive player while running him into a screener.

We coach the man picking off a screen to come so close to the screener that he touches the screener with his hips. This fundamental has to be drilled constantly. There must be no room left between the screener and the man picking so the defense cannot go over the top of the screen. We would like the defense to go behind the screen or jump-switch so that we can end up with a shot or a mismatch.

PICK AND SCREEN

We are very intense about this part of our game. It might get a little rough in practice during the first few weeks. But as a team gets their timing down with the picks and screens, the bumps and blocks turn into precision moves.

A good Pick-and-Screen team will average about one screen foul and one pick foul per season. So a coach can see by these statistics that a team doesn't have to play rough, but they should play with a purposeful intensity. Roughness and fouls are avoided because the screens are usually set in advance. The player taking advantage of a screen has the responsibility of maneuvering his defensive man to a position where he can best pick him off on the screen.

In this system, stationary screens as well as running screens are used. On the stationary screens, the screener puts on the screen as the rule book reads. He assumes a position at the side or in front of a stationary opponent one step away.

The running screen is nothing more than an offensive man running toward a defender while another offensive man is trying to free himself.

The running screen is hard to foul on because the screener would have to bump directly into the opponent. He doesn't blind side anyone, so the opponent sees it coming. The defender tries to avoid the screen by going around it. This is all the time a player needs to receive an open pass or get a good shot.

It's hard for the official to call a foul on the running screen because it takes place away from the ball and the rule book states that the speed of the screener comes into the official's decision; and the position of the screener in this case will vary from one to two normal steps. The key here is to use the running screen *away* from the ball.

Every year we have to wait until the rule book comes out to see if there is a big change in the way our players can screen. Our players must abide by the rule book's interpretation of a legal screen. But there is no rule for an illegal pick. So, the main responsibility of freeing someone for an easy shot is up to the man picking off the screen.

THE BASIC THEORY
OF THE PICK-AND-SCREEN SYSTEM

The first option of the Pick and Screen is to shoot. This is not a run and gun offense. It is a screen, pick, and shoot offense.

We don't believe in assist charts. In this offense, you shoot first, pass second. If a player leads in assists, he didn't do a great job of picking off the screen. If they can't shoot, what else can players do with the ball but set up another player? If a player takes a poor shot and doesn't score, the shooting stats will show that he should have passed the ball to a teammate. We never keep a record of player's assists. We know that this goes against a lot of coaches' theories, but in this system you don't want to overpass.

The biggest coaching problem is keeping the players from passing up a good percentage shot in order to pass to a teammate who might have a tougher shot. Even lay-ups are not good shots for some players. Every member of the team should know the best shooting positions on the floor for each of his teammates.

Helping set up the other player's best shot is our idea of an assist, but that would not necessarily show up on an official stat sheet.

THE LAST-PASS STATISTIC

Instead of the assist statistic, we made up our own stat that would be valuable to judge our players in this type of system. We call it the "last-pass" statistic.

We are interested in finding out who passed the ball to a man who scored. There are assists included in this statistic, but they will not be singled out as an assist. We feel that if a player screens-and-posts, then receives a pass from another player, the passer should get credit for getting the ball into the post man. This will not always be counted as an assist because the post man might have to make some excellent moves to score.

Another example would be found where a player knows another player likes to use a certain screen, so he makes sure that that player gets the ball in that area. After the player receives the pass, he cuts his man off the screen and scores. It's not counted as an assist, but it was the last pass.

Another case would be that our guard knows that our

forward can go one-on-one against his defensive man. The guard then makes sure the forward gets the ball so he can maneuver his man for a drive-in, or a pull-up jump shot. Again, this is not an assist, but the last-pass statistic.

We explain the value of this statistic to our players by comparing a baseball player's batting average to his on-base average. A player might bat .300, but never get on base otherwise. Another player bats .100, but gets on base seven out of every ten times at bat—a .700 on-base average.

Some baseball coaches even use the hard-hit ball statistic instead of hits as a guide to judging their hitter's worth to the team.

We use the last-pass as our method of evaluating our players' activity on the floor. We want the ball to be moved to the right areas.

A player should not try to set a last-pass record. Instead, he should have a balance between his shooting percentage, point production, rebounding, and the last-pass statistics. This will be explained in more detail in Chapter 10.

HOW THE PICK-AND-SCREEN CREATES MISMATCHES KNOWN AS THE "FISH"

We find ourselves every year having one of the smallest teams in our area. We never have all five men that are quick in the same year. We don't have leapers, so we try to create mismatches between our tallest players and one of the opponents' smaller guards (we hope that they have one under 6 feet). Anytime we run through a pick pattern and a switch takes place between a big man and a small man, we holler, "Fish." This tells everyone that there is a mismatch. The bigger man takes the smaller man deep into the "hole" while the other players spread around the court so that the men guarding them cannot sag or switch in order to help out. Diagram 1-1 shows F^1 rolling and posting after screening for G^1. A defensive switch has taken place, so F^1 hollers, "Fish," and the rest of the players move away from F^1 so he can work against the mismatch.

The big man will then post up and someone will try to feed him the ball. Always remember that there is a small man out on the court against a bigger man. The smaller man is also instructed to shoot if his man is sagging to help out. The small man can go one-on-one or feed the big man posting.

If a team is conscious of the "Fish" and it is stressed over and over again, it becomes a great offensive weapon; however, it has to be repeated over and over again in practice.

In one semi-final game in a state tournament against a leaping ball club, that is all our team did on one side of the court. We created a "Fish" with Joe Lentsch, our 6'2" forward, and their 5'10" guard. Joe ended up with 24 points on the "Fish" alone. The "Fish" also brought their leaper (42-inch vertical jump) away from the basket.

The important thing is to make the defense switch by using a tough screen-and-pick. If they don't switch, the guard is able to come around the screen and shoot a jump shot or drive to the basket.

The "Fish" can take place any time in the offense where a switch between a big man and a small man takes place.

By using this mismatch, your team will seem to grow three or four inches during the game.

SCREEN-AND-POST

We are not considered a screen-and-roll team. We do, however, take advantage of the situation if it occurs. We are a screen-and-post team. We hope that there is a switch on the Screen-and-Pick so that we can quick post or call out "Fish" and isolate the opponent's smaller player deep in the post area while we spread out the offense.

With all the weakside defenses being used today, we are stressing more and more the screen-and-post rather than the screen-and-roll.

We also feel that if we go strictly to a roll, the players will have a tendency to pass up their first option of shooting the ball. This quick post move is nothing more than a roll to the basket. When the man rolling gets to a position near the basket, he quickly pivots and works his man on his hip. A normal center posting move is illustrated in Diagram 1-1. This move will be explained in more detail in Chapter 10.

When we use the quick post, we do not holler "Fish," so the remaining players do not spread out around the court. Now the man screening and rolling has the choice of a quick post or a "Fish" call. He alone has that option.

If the pick-and-roll were used, it would have to be against pressure defenses. It would likely happen if the pressure was at half court or more. A guard could hardly pick off a screen and shoot the ball from that distance away from the basket. Not many guards have that kind of range.

In this case, the guard would have to drive, then look for the roll. If he could penetrate close to the basket, then he could look for the quick post. In certain situations we strictly try to create a mismatch. This is only done when one of the opponents has a definite height advantage.

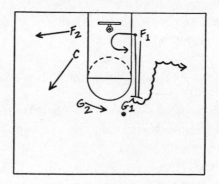

Diagram 1-1
Screen and Post

INTERCHANGING POSITIONS

We also interchange positions during the game (not as a rule, but as the defense dictates). If we feel that another team is just too big for us and if they are blocking a lot of shots inside, we will put our guards at forward or center positions and our forwards or center at the guard position. We don't do this very often, but it has worked for us when we have used it. If their big men are as agile as their guards, then we are in for a real tough game.

One game, when we had to go up against a 6'10" center and our center was 6'3", we put our 5'7" guard at the center position, and our 6'3" center at the guard. We then used some special scissors plays off the high post. This way our center was able to pick his 6'10" defensive man off our 5'7" guard's screen and get some easy lay-ups. We didn't mind if they switched because we were in a good situation for a quick post or "Fish."

We do limit the play selection, however, so that we take most of our shots from under 15 feet away, or we use some special scissors plays off the high post that our big men can handle. We will discuss these plays in Chapter 6.

A player's ability to handle the ball will also determine which player plays what position. We don't want someone in a position that would cut down on his effectiveness. We want this changing of positions to work in our favor.

GUARD MOVEMENT KEYS THE OFFENSE

The direction in which a guard moves after a pass or on the dribble triggers the offense. He calls the plays by the direction he takes after he passes and cuts or by the direction in which he dribbles with the ball.

The center can station himself low, high, or at a side post, as shown in Diagrams 1-2, 1-3, 1-4. If the guard is not overly pressured, he can switch sets with a verbal command by hollering out, "high," "low," or "side." The set can also have a hand signal for one special move on a certain set. By having the guard's movement start our offense, we have eliminated a lot of number calls, hand signals, or the use of cards from the bench. We also use what we call a Double High Post and a Double Low Post as shown in Diagrams 1-5 and 1-6. These are set up by a verbal command from the coach while play is going on or when the ball is dead.

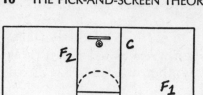

Diagram 1-2
Low Post

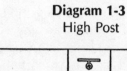

Diagram 1-3
High Post

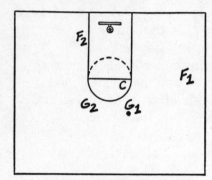

Diagram 1-4
Side Post

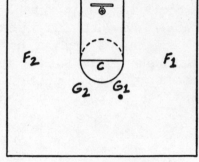

Diagram 1-5
Double High Post

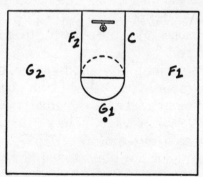

Diagram 1-6
Double Low Post (32 Set)

TYPES OF SCREENS USED
IN THE PICK-AND-SCREEN SYSTEM

1. Outside Screen—Set by F^1 (Diagram 1-7)

2. Inside Screen—Set by F^2 (Diagram 1-7)

3. Spot Screen (Diagram 1-8)
   The screen takes place in a preplanned spot on the floor.
   The man with the ball maneuvers his man to this spot and
   picks him off the screen. This type of screen is used mostly
   when we go back side.

4. Pin Screen (Diagram 1-9)
   This screen is generally used against zones. The idea is to
   pin the defensive man down toward the baseline in order to
   open up a certain area for a shot.

5. Belly-Up Screen
   Facing a man while you are screening him.

6. Back-On Screen
   When a player's back is to the man being screened and he is
   on a certain spot on the floor facing the ball. This way the
   defense doesn't realize that they are being screened until
   the defensive man is picked off. This screen is used on certain plays and against zones.

7. Twin Screen (Diagram 1-10)
   Two players shoulder-to-shoulder when they screen a man
   (Double Screen).

8. Tandem Screen (Diagram 1-11)
   This is a double screen that has one screen after another in a
   line.

9. Running Screen
   The screener runs right at the man so that he has to go
   around him.

10. Radar Screen
    Seeking out the defensive man and adjusting your path of
    the screen. Usually is part of a running screen.

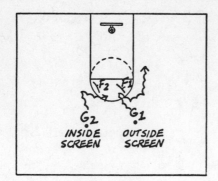

Diagram 1-7

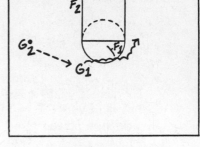

Diagram 1-8
Spot Screen

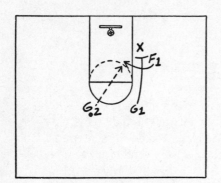

Diagram 1-9
Pin Screen

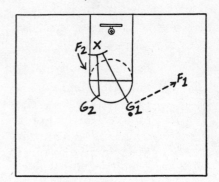

Diagram 1-10
Twin Screen

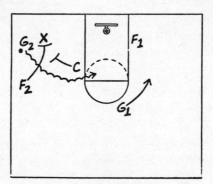

Diagram 1-11
Tandem Screen

Any combination of the screens can be used, for example, a team could use:

a. Spot-Belly-Up Screen
b. Spot-Back-On Screen
c. Radar-Twin Screen
d. Pin-Belly-Up Screen
e. Outside-Spot Screen
f. Inside-Spot Screen

The following chapters will show exactly where to set these screens in order to execute this type of offense.

Included in the Pick-and-Screen theory is a firm belief that any team can screen anywhere on the floor, and pick off any man it wishes to.

INSISTENT COACHING

Once a coach asked us how we teach the Pick-and-Screen. Our answer was that we don't teach it, we demand it.

Our idea of coaching is, that if a player can do everything wrong fundamentally, but can still produce the results, then leave him alone. An exaggerated example would be if a player can shoot the ball from half court and make the shot over 60 percent of the time, we would leave him alone. But if a player (after being coached for some length of time) is still not hitting the 10-foot shot or rebounding the ball after having good position, then we stress the "insistent coaching" method.

We are forceful in our tone when we tell them to "put the ball in the basket," to rebound the ball now to make a good pass. In other words, at this point, we demand the results that accrue from proper execution of the fundamentals. When a player accepts this type of coaching and sees the improvement in his performance, he is going to love the Pick-and-Screen system.

A coach can actually see the improvement over a period of time. Down through the years we have always been noted for our good shooting teams, good rebounding teams, and our Pick-and-Screen teams. We believe 70 percent of our success is credited to our "insistent coaching" method.

During the remainder of the book, we will point out times that you could possibly use this type of coaching. We believe that every successful coach used this method of coaching at least 50 percent of the time. Coaches may not be aware of it, but we believe that all coaches use this type of coaching somewhere in their system.

Insistent coaching is used throughout our system. But because we are talking about our offense, we will relate it only to the Pick-and-Screen offense.

SUMMARY

Basketball fans can identify with a good offensive style of play. Fans identify with the Pick-and-Screen offense. Sometimes we believe that they know as much about the offense as we do.

We have a certain way we want our players to shoot. We also limit their shot selections to good percentage shots. This shot selection is built into the offense. We believe this is why we are always known as a good shooting team.

Rebounding positions are also built right into the offense. We also believe this is why we are known for our good rebounding teams, despite our very average heights and weights.

Discipline in knowing where and when to shoot and rebound makes an average ball player look like an all-stater.

We feel that we are a type of team that shoots the ball and storms the boards. If a team gets a lot of inside shots blocked because they are overmatched in height, then that team can rely on this offense to help them take tight perimeter shots. A team can also free their smaller forwards by double screening for them so they can shoot a jump shot inside without getting every shot blocked.

If a coach has developed a player to a certain level and it still is not good enough to execute his system, then he should use the insistent coaching technique.

We let our players know that they have two coaches during a game, their coach and the other team's coach. We feel that if we screen and pick a man for an easy basket, the other coach usually calls time out or hollers out to his players to fight through the screens. This is the time that we can adjust our picks to work in our favor.

We have won a lot of games over the years using this offense and we will win a lot more.

We have a lot of Picks-and-Screens and a lot of sets, but we run basically the same thing all the time. The next few chapters will show you the entire playbook.

2

BUILDING THE LOW POST OFFENSE WITH THE PICK-AND-SCREEN

In this chapter, the low post plays are explained and diagrammed. However, the actual technical fundamentals needed to run the Pick-and-Screen offense will be discussed in a later chapter.

This is the main offense. Every other thing that is done comes off this concept. Remember at all times that the players should shoot first, pass second. A good thing to remember while reading about this offense is the passing and movement of the guards. The guards are the quarterbacks of the offense. The forward has the option of screening directly on the guards' defensive man if he feels he can roll and post on his man before the guards look for him breaking to a wing position. With these two thoughts in mind, let's get on with the offense.

All moves that are diagrammed to one side are also duplicated on the other side of the court.

The offense starts when the players are in position, as shown in Diagram 2-1. Note that the guards are at the top of the key and the free throw sidelines extended. F^1 is ready to make a V-cut of some kind. Player G^1 has the choice of passing the ball either to F^1 or F^2 (who is now breaking up to the center of the free throw line). If G^1 passes to F^2 as he arrives above the line (Diagram 2-2), G^2 will back door. (We call this the peek play because we feel that the defensive guard on G^2 will take a peek at the ball when it is passed to F^2.) Player F^1 is also making his move toward the basket at this time to pick his man off the center as shown in Diagram 2-2.

The first option for F^2 is to pass the ball to G^2 if he is open for a lay-up. Player G^1 at this time is driving his man down to the free throw lane extended and is now ready to cut across in front of F^2 as illustrated in Diagram 2-2. Player G^1 drives his man down first to set up his defensive man for a better picking angle.

Whether the ball is passed to F^2 or not, the play is on. There will be times when G^2 will be so open that G^1 can pass the ball over the top of F^2 directly to G^2 for a lay-up. Player G^2 makes his move as soon as F^2 is above the free throw line. If G^1 cannot pass to G^2 or F^2, he drives his man deep with the dribble and then he cuts back in front of F^2. He uses F^2 as a screen and picks his man off him. His first option is to drive to the basket. If the drive is not there, he has the option of shooting at S, as shown in Diagram 2-3.

The coaching point here is: If G^1 knows that his man continually goes behind the screen by F^2 rather than over the top, he can stop at S and jump shoot or continue picking off F^2 back and forth until he is open for a shot (Diagram 2-3). Player F^2 at this time has opened up his stance to take up more room on the screen. He should execute a tough, belly-up screen. Player F^2 will face G^1 each time he goes from one side to the other.

If G^1 does not have the drive to the basket, he pulls up and tries to back off with the dribble and looks for F^1 who has picked his man off the center. By backing off, G^1 doesn't lose his dribble and allows more room for F^1 to post deep.

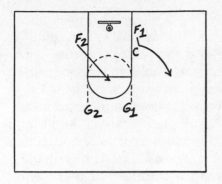

Diagram 2-1

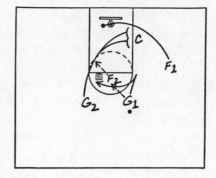

Diagram 2-2

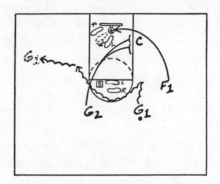

Diagram 2-3

The coaching point here is: The center does not use a belly-up screen on the man guarding F^1. Instead, he uses a back-on screen by opening up to the ball side, and F^1 uses him to pick his man off (Diagram 2-3). The back-on screen is used so that the defensive man on F^1 does not realize that the center is a screener, but most important is the fact that the defensive center is looking at the ball and cannot help with a switch. The defensive center is actually a screener by taking up room in that area.

Player F^1 continues on and receives a screen from G^2 just past the basket. It is very important that the screen and pick take place on the other side of the basket away from the ball so that F^1 can post as deep as possible. Player G^2 actually runs toward the defensive man and makes him go around him.

Notice that in Diagram 2-3, G^2 will be screening below or above the center, depending on whether the defensive man on F^1 is trying to go over the top or behind the center's screen.

The F^1 picks off the two screens and comes to a position just on the other side of the basket and wraps his leg around his man keeping him on his back as shown in Diagram 2-3. There will be times when F^1 is completely free to shoot and other times the man guarding him will be delayed enough that F^1 will have an excellent deep posting position. At this time, G^1 will feed him the ball for an easy turn-around shot after having previously wrapped his leg and pivoted directly toward the basket.

If F^1 is covered because the defensive guard on G^2 is hanging underneath, then G^1 looks for G^2 who, after his screen, continued to his next position (Diagram 2-4). Player G^1 will pass to G^2 for a short jump shot. If the passing lane to G^2 is not open because the forward on F^2 is sagging, then G^1 will pass to F^2, who may shoot or pass the ball to G^2.

If F^2 receives the ball as in Diagram 2-2, and he cannot get the ball to G^2 for the peek, he can either wait to hand off to G^1 or fake the hand-off, turn and shoot, or hit F^1, who has wrapped his leg around his man. He could also hit G^2 coming from behind the center. Remember, F^2 has the first option to *shoot*, and then pass.

You will find that if you have a strong forward, your guard G^1 will be able to pass directly to him at the free throw line to

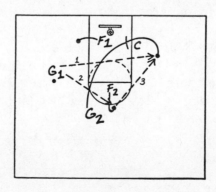

Diagram 2-4

start the play. You will also get a lot out of the peek play and will often feed forward F^1 as he wraps his leg around his man.

If G^1 is a strong guard, he will usually get a lay-up drive after he picks his man off F^2. If a team is blessed with a quick guard, he will get a lot of jump shots after he picks off F^2.

If the defensive center is constantly moving over to the ball side to help with F^1, the center and forward can set up their own verbal signals between them. This tells the center to take advantage of this situation by cutting directly across the lane for a short jump shot as shown in Diagram 2-5. This usually keeps the defensive center honest.

The best way to handle this material is to picture yourself in a certain position and go through the whole pattern. Let's say you are G^1 with the ball. You've just brought the ball quickly up the court and worked it so that you are level with the top of the key. Player F^1 makes a V-cut to receive the ball from you. Player F^2 has also made his move to the top of the free throw line at the center. You can't pass to either of them, because they are both closely guarded, so you look for G^2, who has made his move to the basket. You cannot see him open (over the top), so you dribble deep, finally cutting back in front of F^2. Player F^2 at this time is now facing you for a belly-up screen. At this time, F^1 is making his move to pick his man off the center. The center is now facing the ball side, using a back-on screen. As you cut across in front of F^2, you are looking for a quick jump shot but instead you see an opening toward the

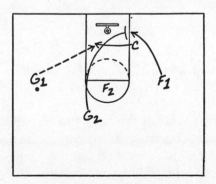

Diagram 2-5

basket. As you start the drive, someone fills the lane so you cannot drive. You pull up and back off a couple of steps with the dribble and you look for F^1 coming around the center and also picking his man off G^2. Player F^1 is now wrapping his leg around his defensive man. The defensive man on G^2 switches men so you look for G^2 continuing around the center's screen. He is covered so he continues to the top of the key. You pass him the ball and he is on his way for a back-side pick.

Notice how the patterns determine movement *away from the ball* and how they define the other players' moves, yet not in a defined, predictable pattern. Rather, the offense is filled with defined options within a basic pattern.

If a team continually ends up with a back-side pick, they are not doing the job on their picks and screens. Remember, it isn't the technique of the screen and pick that is important, but the willingness of a player to step in front of a moving man. The technique is the timing of the screen so that a player is set as close as possible to the man he wants to screen without fouling him. The man picking should touch his hip against the screener as he goes by him. We average only one foul per season on our screens and picks, and only one lane violation (on our guard screening on the peek play) per season. These statistics verify the theory that the screens and picks can be mastered without worrying about fouls and lane violations because of poor timing.

PICK BACK SIDE

We have referred previously to the back-side pick, so it would be a good time to explain what is meant by this before we go on to other situations. This is sort of a follow-through to the offense.

If some play does not work to one side of the court, a team has two choices; either they set up again, or they go back side. We like to go back side because we feel that some of the best screens and picks take place with this move. Let's say that the peek play is being run and all the options are taken away.

Player G^2 will quickly break to the top of the key and receive a pass from G^1. He then goes back side, as we like to do on every play that doesn't materialize, and gets a screen from the center as shown in Diagram 2-6. If nothing comes of this, the ball can go to the back side again (to G^1) and he can get a screen by F^1.

If a team has two quick guards, it could make this an entire offense. When I had Paul Molitor, now playing with the Milwaukee Brewers, playing a guard position in this offense, he used the back-side type of move most of the time. The other guard, Jerry Boland, was also extremely quick, so they would go back and forth until one or the other would get a jump shot or a drive to the basket. From now on, when we refer to going back side, this is the move we'll be talking about.

DOUBLE SCREEN GUARD IN THE CORNER

This play is started from the low post lineup shown in Diagram 2-7. Player F^1 makes a V-cut to receive the ball. Player G^1 passes to F^1 and breaks for the basket as the center is moving up to screen for G^1. G^1 picks his man off the center and if he is open as he moves directly to the basket he will receive a pass from F^1. If he is not open, G^1 will continue deep toward the baseline before he makes his cut to the center shown in Diagram 2-7. Player F^1 passes the ball to G^1 and sets a screen for him. Player

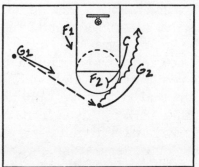

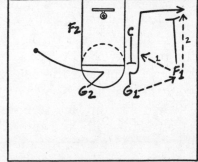

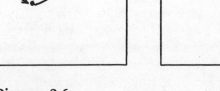

Diagram 2-6   **Diagram 2-7**

G^1 then picks his man off F^1, who will not roll to the basket, but will stay at the screen position for a possible return pass. The center will now move over to get in position to set the second screen for G^1 (Diagram 2-8). At this time, G^2 will fade out to give G^1 more room.

If G^1 decides that the defensive center is switching all the time, he can hit the center with the ball as he rolls to the basket, as shown in Diagram 2-9. We tell the guards that the defensive center, after the switch, will follow him to the center of the free throw line. After that, the defensive center will start to worry about where his man went and he will start to back off to help with the center. This will hold up 95 percent of the time. The guards are coached to be patient with this and to take any high percentage shots anywhere along their dribble paths. At times, the defensive guard on G^2 will come over to help, so G^1 will pass to G^2 (Diagram 2-9), who in turn will get a pick from F^2. If nothing comes of this, we either set up again or go back side.

GUARD SPECIAL—OPTION i

This play gives the defensive team fits. If a team has a clever guard, this is his play. Diagram 2-10 depicts the start of the play, which looks like a double pick in the corner. Player G^2 passes the ball to F^1, who has freed himself with a V-cut for the pass. Player G^1 starts down toward the baseline as he always does, again picking his man off the center, who is moving up. If G^1 is open he gets the pass, otherwise he stops low and faces the forward. This is the key for the guard special to be run. In the previous play, G^1 broke to the center; now he stays low. Player F^1 will feed the ball to the center and run right at G^1, who at this time runs away from him under the basket until he touches the opposite free throw lane marker. Player G^1 then reverses his path to eventually receive a pass from the center for a jump shot. In the meantime, the center is dribbling the ball while shuffling toward the spot G^1 has occupied, as shown in Diagram 2-11. Player G^2 at this time is moving to his position at the center of the free throw line. The center is dribbling with

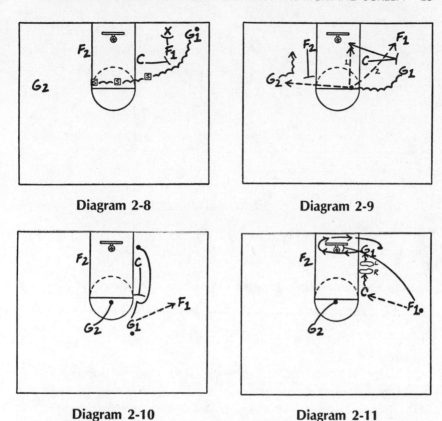

Diagram 2-8   Diagram 2-9

Diagram 2-10   Diagram 2-11

his back to the lane and in the direction of the baseline. Player F^1 will screen as close to the basket as he can. While G^1 is reversing his path he picks his man off F^1, then picks again if necessary off the center, who has left just enough room between himself and the baseline for G^1 to come around and receive the ball.

The center gives the ball to G^1, who has a short jump shot. If G^1 feels that the defensive player is right on his heels, he continues around the center for a shot in front of the basket or anything else that might develop at this time (Diagram 2-12).

Player G^2 is at the free throw position at the start of the play in case the forward runs at G^1. As the center is shuffling down with the dribble, the defensive player on G^2 may try to steal the ball by doubling on the center. This happens quite

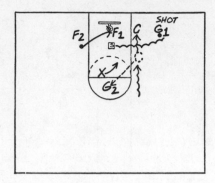

Diagram 2-12

often, as shown in Diagram 2-12. Player G² at this time would holler "ball—ball," and the center would pass it to G² for an easy jump shot.

If the defense is taking the guard special away, F¹ can run at G² instead. This is another double pick, first off F¹ and then the center (Diagram 2-13). After G² receives the ball he can drive to the basket or take a jump shot when and where he likes to.

Note that G¹ runs underneath the basket whether he is in the play or not. If F¹ runs at G², then G¹ does not reverse his path, but continues out to get in a safety position.

Again, if nothing happens, the ball is reversed to the back side or the team will reset.

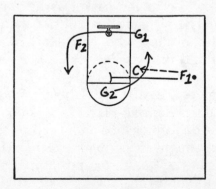

Diagram 2-13

GUARD SPECIAL—CENTER POP—OPTION II

When the guard special is being run, the center has two options. He can receive the pass from a post up position as in Option I, or he can pop out to a guard position as shown in Diagram 2-14.

Player G^1 passes to F^1 and moves to a deep post position as he does in Option I. The center decides not to post up, but breaks out to a guard position to receive the pass from F^1. After F^1 passes to the center, F^1 runs right at G^1, who at this time runs away from F^1 under the basket until his foot touches the opposite free throw lane marker. Player G^1 then reverses his path and picks his man off of F^1's screen (Diagram 2-14).

Option II should be used when the other team is taking away the pass from F^1 to the center in his Option I post position. If the defensive center is exceptionally tall, this is a good chance to bring him away from the basket. The center is also coached and instructed to shoot from that outside area if the defensive center is sagging. The center must not break out so far that he is out of his shooting range. The center should always be a shooting threat. If he breaks out of his shooting range, the defense can sag and the play would not be as effective.

When G^2 sees G^1 setting up a guard special, G^2 moves to the free throw line as he did in Option I. If the center breaks out

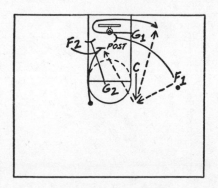

Diagram 2-14

to the guard position, G^2 moves down and screens for F^2, who comes around the screen in a deep post position (Diagram 2-14). The center is instructed to look for F^2 first because of the slow development of the guard special play. If F^2 is not open, he breaks up to the guard position. The center then looks for the options created by G^1 and F^1. Another reason we want G^2 and F^2 to work together is to create movement on the back side so the defense cannot use any back-side help. Actually F^2, after he breaks up to the guard spot, has enough time to change positions with G^2 a second time and help with the rebounding if he doesn't receive a pass and go back side (Diagram 2-15).

There are so many options shown in Diagram 2-14 and 2-15 that a team could actually run an entire offense off the guard special.

After receiving the ball, the first option for F^1 always is to shoot. He can also feed G^1 who posts up. He can pass to the center who has broken out to the guard position and then screen for G^1. Player G^1 could fake coming around the screen and peek back to the basket. Player F^1, after screening for G^1, can pivot immediately and do a quick post deep in the lane as illustrated in Diagram 2-15.

If G^1 receives the pass from the center after picking off F^1's screen and can't get a shot off, G^1 can feed F^1 in a deep side posting position as shown in Diagram 2-15.

Furthermore, when the center has the ball, he could shoot from the guard position, or he can feed F^1 who posts deep. In

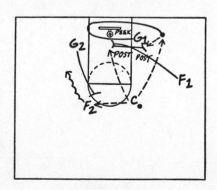

Diagram 2-15

addition, he can feed F^2 who posts deep after using the screen by G^2. The center could also feed F^2 as he posts and then breaks up to the guard position. Player F^2 could shoot from that position or feed G^2, who posts. If it isn't there, G^2 and F^2 could work a back-side screen-and-pick.

FORWARD SPECIAL

We use this play when we want the forward to get involved in the scoring. It's another way for a team to change positions on a certain play. It is a play that can be used when the defense is pressuring the forward and G^1 cannot pass the ball to F^1 in the wing position.

This play is the same as the guard special except that instead of G^1 passing to F^1, he dribbles toward him. This is the key that lets the entire team know the forward special play is on. As G^1 dribbles toward F^1, F^1 will run toward the basket until he reaches the free throw lane. When his foot touches the lane marker, he pivots and posts up (Diagram 2-16).

We purposely have the center in Diagram 2-16 on the opposite side of the lane to point out that a team reads the guard's movement (in this case, G^1 dribbling toward F^1), and that no matter where the center is lined up, he knows that this is the key to get to a post position to run the forward special.

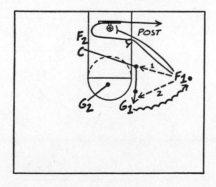

Diagram 2-16

When F^1 posts up, G^1 will try to feed him. If he cannot, he looks for the center in the higher post position. Player G^1 passes to the center and runs right at F^1, who then runs away and cuts back using G^1's screen and simultaneously the center's screen as it was explained in the guard special play.

This play was put in to take the pressure off the guards when they were trying to pass to a forward who was being pressured. It was so effective that we decided to put it in our playbook. We now run it any time the pressure is there or any time we want to. It has become an important part of our offense.

FORWARD SPECIAL—CENTER POP

The only difference between this move and the forward special is that the center breaks up to the guard position to receive the ball from G^1. All the options after that are the same as the "guard special" play.

OVER-THE-TOP PICK

Player G^1 again starts the play. He passes to F^1 and follows his pass, as shown in Diagram 2-17. This is the key for the center to move up and F^2 to move up higher than the center. At the time

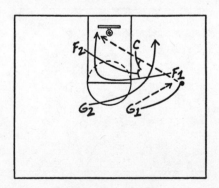

Diagram 2-17

this is happening, G^2 breaks around and picks his man off F^2. If G^2 is open, the ball can be passed to him, but the big play is hitting F^1 over the top (Diagram 2-17). Player G^1 tries to lay the ball up as close to the basket as he can so F^1 can catch the ball in the air and shoot it before he comes down. Some teams refer to this as the "alley-oop."

Player F^2 is coached to keep it nice and tight to the center so that no defensive man can get between them. Players F^2 and the center also get their arms up and holler for the ball as they set their screens. This keeps their defensive men on them tightly so that they cannot sag and help on the eventual lob pass to F^1.

Player G^1, after receiving the ball back from F^1, looks for an over-the-top pass to F^1. If he sees anyone sagging off to help, he passes to that open man. If F^2 or the center receives the ball, he turns and looks for the shot. If his man comes back on him, he can pass off to F^1. Either way, the play works fine.

This is a pretty play that a lot of teams use. If it cannot be executed, G^2 can break to the corner and get a tandem screen, or F^2 can screen for G^1 as he dribbles toward him. Player F^1 can also come up to set a second screen (Diagram 2-18).

The key to getting this play started is the guard passing to F^1 and going over to get the ball back. This key starts everyone going to their new positions.

GUARD DEEP PICK (Diagram 2-19)

Player G^1 this time breaks behind the center and comes out to receive a pass from F^1. When G^1 catches the ball, the center goes down and screens for him. Player F^1 fades out to the baseline in case his defensive man tries to drop off to help out.

Player G^1 picks his man off the center and shoots a jump shot or he continues around the center for a shot in the middle of the lane, as shown in Diagram 2-19.

Remember, F^1 has to make a break for the baseline so his defensive man cannot sag to help out. However, if the defensive man on F^1 drops off to help, G^1 can pass the ball to F^1 for a jump shot.

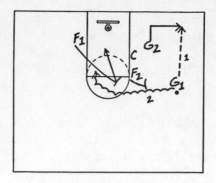

Diagram 2-18

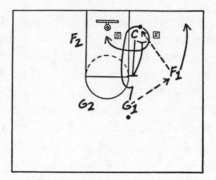

Diagram 2-19

QUICK SHUFFLE PICK

Player G^1 has the ball and cannot pass the ball to F^1. Player F^2 did not break to the free throw line for the peek play, so G^1 passes to G^2. The center still breaks up as he always does. Player G^1 this time breaks toward the basket with the idea of screening the defensive man on F^1 if that man decides to go behind the center. The center faces back side and is in a position to screen for F^1. The center is less likely to use a moving screen if his back is to F^1.

As G^2 receives the ball, F^1 will pick his man off the center. At this time, it would be better for G^2 to pass the ball to F^1, as shown in Diagram 2-20. But if it cannot be executed, G^2 will pass the ball to F^2 and he will try to pass to F^1.

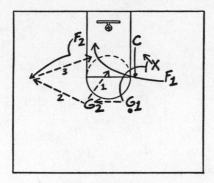

Diagram 2-20

Player G^2 has the better pass to F^1 because the defensive center is still one pass away from the ball, so it would be less likely that he would sag to cut off the shuffle move.

Again, if the play doesn't work, the team will reset or go back side. If F^1 is good at posting up, he can do this if he doesn't receive the pass; or G^2 can make a quick break for the corner and have F^2 and F^1 set up the double tandem screen in the corner for G^2.

OPEN SIDE OFFENSE

We consider the open side of the court the side with only two players on it, as shown in Diagram 2-21. Player G^2 has taken

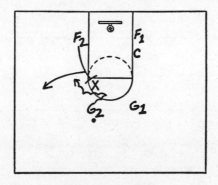

Diagram 2-21

the ball down the court and is ready to start two-on-two basketball with F^2. The forward can come up and put a screen on X^2 or he can make a V-cut to receive a pass toward the sideline. G^2 can pass to F^2 and screen for him, or they can just keep working together until one or the other is open for a short jump shot. We spend a lot of time with this during our drills (see Chapter 11). Player G^1 is patient, as are F^1 and the center. They watch for an opening to the basket if their men are sagging to the open side. They are also waiting for a return pass to G^1 so they can go to the back-side offense.

If at any time G^2 breaks for the corner or a deep spot by the lane, the double pick in the corner is on, or the guard special can be run (Diagram 2-22). The center is ready to come across the lane for both moves: to either receive the ball for the guard special or to set up the double screen for the guard. If G^2 wants to run the peek play, he has to wave the center over to his side of the court.

The open side offense is used late in ball games or if we have players that are good with two-on-two basketball.

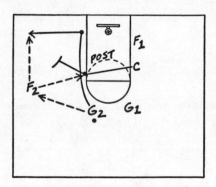

Diagram 2-22

CLOSED SIDE OFFENSE

The closed side offense is the side with three players on it. While in this set, the following plays are used:

   a. Guard special
   b. Forward special

c. Double screen in corner
d. Guard deep pick
e. Scissor pick

The scissor pick is worked with the center, guard, and forward. Player G^1 passes to F^1 but doesn't make any kind of move. This is the key for the center to post up high and receive the ball from F^1 (Diagram 2-23). After passing the ball, F^1 will cut by the center, leaving just enough room so the player guarding him can't go over the top of the center's screen. Player F^1 will then screen for G^1. At this time, G^1 is driving his man as deep into the lane as necessary so that he can pick his man off F^1 and then off the center. Player G^1 receives a hand-off from the center for a quick jump shot or a drive to the basket.

Player G^1 can also pass to F^1 and fade out across the lane. This side then becomes the open side and two-on-two basketball by the center and forward is set up (Diagram 2-24).

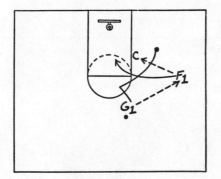

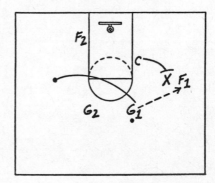

Diagram 2-23   Diagram 2-24

Let's catch our breath for awhile and remember what we are trying to do. We want to shoot first, pass second. There are a lot of diagrams, but remember that this is our playbook.

Some years we use all of it and other years we hand pick what we need to match our personnel. In this offense, there is something for everyone. For instance, this past year one of our guards had great success with the "guard special," so he ran it all the time.

It is also important to notice the players' movement without the ball. For instance, as F^2 moves up to start the peek play, but G^1 decides to pass to F^1 instead, F^2 will just move back to his original position to rebound or wait for something else to develop. The players are coached to try any play they want, and then to look for the many options that the offense creates. We let the best players run the offense and have some fun "picking" the defense apart, piece by piece, pick by pick.

The other guard handled the double screen in the corner as well as any guard we had, so he didn't have to be reminded that the play was there any time he wanted to use it.

There is also another great reason for using this set system. It's called rebounding. We know where our ball players are at all times, so we know who rebounds where on every move.

3

DEVELOPING PICKS AND SCREENS
OFF THE HIGH POST

The high post was the second set we put into our playbook. The low post was allowing the forwards to get shots in a deep post position with their backs to the basket. We needed a way to free the forwards so that they could take shots while facing the basket. This would make them more of a triple threat. We also wanted these shots to be good percentage shots and to be close to the basket, and we wanted the guards to continue to get free for lay-ups and short jump shots. Everything in this offensive set is geared to take shots in the boundary of the free throw lane.

We must give credit at this time to Duane Baglien, the former coach of the great Edina, Minnesota teams of the late 1960s. Our team had the pleasure of scrimmaging his teams during the years Edina was setting a state record of 69 consecutive victories and three straight Minnesota State Championships. Duane talked us into using a high post to go along with our low post attack.

After we decided to use a high post, the next thing was to stay within our own philosophy of the Pick-and-Screen. We had to make sure that the guards were not duplicating their moves so that the rest of the team would know what was going on, so we added some unique moves for the guards that would key the plays being used. We also found a way to blend in the low post plays.

GUARD SCISSOR PICK

Diagram 3-1 depicts the players in position to start the high post. Player F^1 has already made his V-cut to receive a pass at the wing position. At all times, keep in mind the cut used by G^1 after he passes to F^1. It will trigger the offense to run a certain play. The center will always keep his eye on G^1. If G^1 scissors, the center will do what G^1 does.

Player G^1 passes the ball to F^1, then cuts to a position on the right side of the center, stops, and hesitates one count. While G^1 is moving to his position, G^2 picks his man off G^1 by cutting as close as possible to him. Player G^2 will also use the center as a screener as he heads directly for the basket as shown in Diagram 3-1.

If G^2 is open, he will receive a pass from F^1 for a lay-up. We want G^2 to cut as tight as he can and try to stay inside the free throw lane for a quick lay-up (Diagram 3-2). We emphasize G^2 staying inside the free throw lane because sometimes the guard cuts too far outside of the lane and has to shoot a longer shot than we would like him to. The outside type of cut also

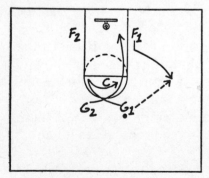

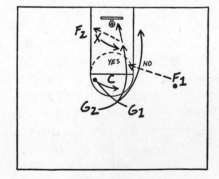

Diagram 3-1   Diagram 3-2

gives the defensive man a chance to recover and catch up to G^2.

The only defensive man that could give back-side help to cover G^2 is the man guarding F^2. Player G^2 is coached to pass to F^2 if this occurs, and F^2 goes in for the lay-up shown in Diagram 3-2.

GUARD AROUND PICK

This is a continuation move from the guard scissor. Player G^1 passes the ball and makes his scissor cut. If F^1 cannot feed the ball to G^2 as he scissors, then F^1 will look for G^1 coming around the center (Diagram 3-3). This situation usually occurs when the defensive guards switch. Notice in Diagram 3-3 that if G^2 doesn't get the ball, he keeps on coming around to get into position to screen, and then moves upcourt. From there he can go back side, or, if G^1 shoots, he can help rebound or become a safety man.

When G^1 receives the ball, he looks for a jump shot right away without wasting time with a dribble. The center at this time faces G^1 and opens up his stance with his feet a little wider than shoulder width (Diagram 3-4). We have the center get into a good belly-up screening position because if G^1 cannot get the shot off, he will use the center's screen and pick his man off as he goes to the other side of the free throw line for a jump shot (Diagram 3-4). Player G^1 can actually go back and forth until he is open for a shot. All the center has to do is turn around and

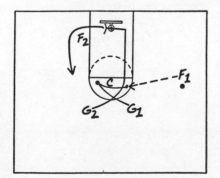

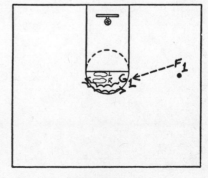

Diagram 3-3   **Diagram 3-4**

face G^1 so that he can pick his man again as G^1 comes back to his original position.

The only way the defensive guard can stop the initial pass to G^1 is to overplay him toward the ball and anticipate G^1 coming back for the ball. If this happens, the guard is instructed to go in back of the center to receive the pass (Diagram 3-5). This move usually keeps the defense honest.

GUARD AND CENTER DOUBLE SCREEN FORWARD

Player G^1 passes to F^1 and cuts past the center away from the ball. The play looks like the guard scissor, but instead of G^1 stopping next to the center, he continues down toward the basket to screen for F^2 (Diagram 3-6). The center's rule is to go where the guard goes so he also heads down to screen for F^2.

The actual technique of double screening and using the screen to pick off is explained in Chapter 10.

As the double screen (twin screen) gets there, F^2 makes a baseline fake and uses a quick move around the screen in picking his man off and moving directly toward the ball to receive a pass. The forward (F^2) should go all the way in for a lay-up, but if he can't, he has a short jump shot in the free throw lane for an excellent percentage shot. Returning to the opening pass for G^1 to F^1, F^1 could still feed G^2 the ball if he is open on the

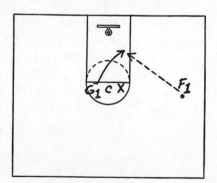

Diagram 3-5

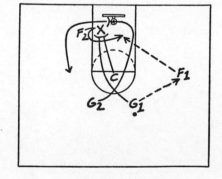

Diagram 3-6

scissors. If G^2 doesn't receive the ball, he keeps moving away from the ball, leaving enough room between himself and the baseline for F^2 to use him for a screen if F^2 decides to go low instead of over the top of the twin screen. Whether G^2 becomes a screener or not, he continues on to a safety position (Diagram 3-6).

GUARDS' DOUBLE SCREEN ON THE FORWARD

Player G^1 has the ball and passes to F^1. Player G^1 then cuts past the center on the ball side and heads toward F^2, as shown in Diagram 3-7. The center follows the guard and times his move so that he can use G^1 as a screen; he then slides down toward the basket looking for the ball and a lay-up.

Player G^2 starts his normal scissor cut, but sees the key of G^1 cutting on the ball side, so he goes directly down to help set up a twin screen with G^1. The center should receive the ball at this time because he has a quick slide to the basket for an easy lay-up. If he doesn't receive the ball, he will cut away from the ball to set up a screen for F^2 if F^2 decides to go underneath the twin screen. In either case, the center will rebound away from the ball.

The guards' double screen on the forward is the second most productive play off the high post. We wish that we would

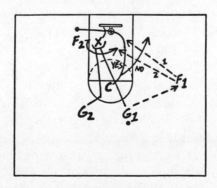

Diagram 3-7

have kept stats on how many baskets we have scored over the
years on this particular play. We know it has been a gold mine.
While this play is developing, F^1 has the first option (as in all
our plays), which is to shoot or drive to the basket. It can be
noticed in Diagram 3-7 that the lane is open to the baseline for
F^1. If F^1 is a good driving forward, he would most likely accept
the second option of driving to the basket one-on-one if his
man is playing him tough. If F^2 goes over the top of the twin
screen, he is not effecting the baseline drive of F^1.

When G^1 makes his cut by the center, he does not stop to
screen for the center but cuts as close to the center as he possibly can. The center opens up to the ball and steps around G^1 as
he passes by and keeps facing F^1 as he shuffles to the basket. In
this way, the center can protect the ball with his back should
the man guarding him recover. The center then has him on
either his hip or his back when he receives the ball as he goes in
for a lay-up. However, the center must try to slide inside the
free throw lane (Diagram 3-7). This makes the play more effective by its quickness to the basket and keeps the defensive man
from making a quick recovery.

FORWARD "POP" OFF—OPTION I

As G^2 scissors and continues to a safety position for defensive
purposes, he leaves enough room between himself and the
baseline for F^2 to come around on what is called the forward
"Pop" (Diagram 3-8). Player G^2 is actually setting a running
screen if he sees F^2 coming around deep.

Player F^2 uses his "Pop" option when he finds that his
defensive man is always anticipating a double screen (twin)
and is trying to fight through it by meeting it higher up the
court. While this defensive man is working hard to get
through, F^2 starts up like he is going to use the screen, but cuts
back to use the running screen by G^2 (Diagram 3-8).

This always is a great play, but is especially good late in a
game when a team needs a good counter play. The threat of F^2
going over the top of the twin screen or popping underneath
puts a lot of pressure on the defensive man guarding F^2.

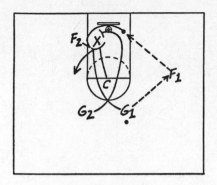 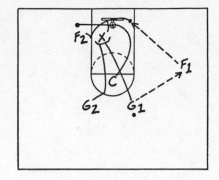

Diagram 3-8   **Diagram 3-9**

FORWARD "POP" OFF—OPTION II

The forward "Pop" can be used with the guards' twin screen on the forward. The center will use a running screen to free F^2 and will then go to the opposite side of the lane to rebound (Diagram 3-9).

Player F^2 can run the forward "Pop" whenever he wants to. But if he is having success going over the top of the twin screen, then he should save this move until a key basket is needed in a game. The defense at this time would most likely be looking for F^2 coming over the top of the screen.

GUARD "POP"

This manuever is mostly a counter play and is set up during a time out or a dead ball situation. It comes off the "Guards' Double Screen on the Forward" play.

We find that during the course of a game, the player guarding G^2 follows him down only part way. Ninety-nine percent of the time it will be the man guarding G^2 who gets in the way of the forward by plugging up the middle.

In this situation we call a time-out and we plan the strategy of popping G^2 around and out for a quick shot (Diagram 3-10). After a team does this once, and especially if they score

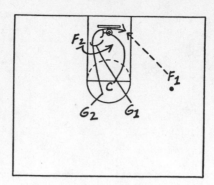

Diagram 3-10

on it, they should have no more trouble with the defensive guard plugging up the middle.

Player F^1 should not use his option of driving in this case because we are looking for G^2 deep. If F^1's defensive man is sagging, he still has the option of shooting or looking for F^2 if G^2 is not open for some reason.

All the counter plays are set up as early in a game as needed so we can dictate our offense the rest of the game.

HIT THE CENTER

Player G^1 passes the ball to the center. After he catches the ball, the center pivots and faces the basket and looks for F^2, who steps quickly into the free throw lane. It is important for the center to face the basket so that he is a scoring threat to shoot or drive. Player F^2 makes a quick post move and tries to get the defensive man on his hip by wrapping his left leg in front of the defensive man (Diagram 3-11).

The only reason F^2 would not be able to receive the pass is that the man guarding him would be playing halfway in front of him. Notice that in Diagram 3-11, G^2 started to move to a position that is even with the free throw line extended. By making this move, the guard prevents his defensive man from helping out on the center. Another reason is that if the center cannot pass the ball to F^2 because of the defensive man's over-

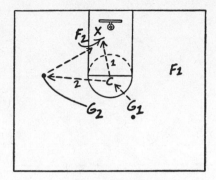

Diagram 3-11

play on F^2, then the center would pass the ball to G^2, who passes to F^2 for a power lay-up or an over-the-top pass (Diagram 3-11).

The key here is to have G^2 fade away and look for a pass from the center. A quick pass to G^2 and G^2's pass to F^2 cause the defensive man guarding F^2 to try to get new position. While he is trying to get a better position, the ball is passed to F^2. If F^2 is being fronted, there is plenty of room to pass over the top.

DOUBLE HIGH POST

The only difference between this set and the normal high post is the positioning of the forward F^2 away from the ball (Diagram 3-12).

The name of this set might be misleading, but to us we have two men high that we didn't have in the low post set. This is the reason it is called the "Double High Post."

This set is used for three reasons:

1. If the other team is just too big for the forwards to manuever around at a deep position, then our forwards take them farther away from the basket.
2. If the defense is denying the pass from G^1 to the center, than there is more room to throw over the top—this is called the "center peek."

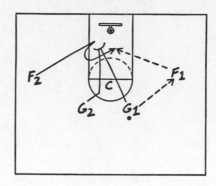

Diagram 3-12

3. If we are playing a team that uses a lot of back-side help to stop the high post plays, this set would spread them out and neutralize their back-side help.

In this set, every play off the normal high post is used. As soon as the ball is passed to F^1, F^2 will start working his way down toward the basket (Diagram 3-12). This will prevent the man guarding F^2 from having any time to step over and give back-side help on the scissor plays. The defensive man is also concerned by the possibility of F^2 being double screened for a shot. Besides the advantage of having an open space under the basket, it adds a little more movement to the "Double Screen on the Forward" play shown in Diagram 3-12.

If the defensive center is overplaying the ball side, then it would be a good time to go into the double high post. When G^1 sees the overplay, he fakes a pass to the center, who then peeks to the basket (alley-oop pass). The actual signals used are discussed in Chapter 6 when we talk about pressure defenses, and again in Chapter 10.

One year we ran the double high post most of the season because our forwards were 5'11" and 5'10". It sure worked to our advantage. We did, however, run our other sets, but when we wanted to run a high post, we went to the double high.

SWITCHING POSITIONS

A team can switch any player to any position desired with the high post. We actually made this discovery accidentally. Our season was going along just fine, so one day at practice we decided to have a little fun. We let the forwards have their big dream of playing guard and let the guards have their dream of being great post men and rebounders. As it turned out, the offense worked great. The thing we were most excited with was the way the forwards could score off the scissor plays. Even the center, who had to take his turn at guard, was enjoying his scoring opportunities. The guards adjusted to their new role as forwards. They were either breaking out to a wing position or they were rebounding against someone their own size. The guards also liked it when the two big men came down to set a twin screen so that the guard could score. This "switch" gave each player a better understanding and appreciation of the other players' responsibilities on certain plays.

We therefore decided to put this in our playbook and we have used it on many occasions in big situations.

A team would switch positions for four reasons:

1. To take advantage of the opponent's big man by taking him away from the basket.
2. To make use of some special skills that one of the players might have.
3. To take advantage of the opponent's worst defensive player.
4. To show the other team a new look and force them to make adjustments.

For example, if the man guarding F^2 was not very mobile, we would switch F^2 to G^2's spot and run the guard scissor (Diagram 3-13).

Remember that players can be placed in any position where it gives your team the advantage. In a state tournament game, we were short of guards because of injuries and foul

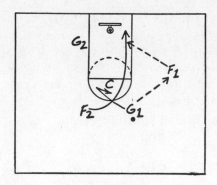

Diagram 3-13

trouble. We put the best forward reserve where F^2 is lined up in Diagram 3-13. He had a field day on the scissor play and also on our guard around play. We weren't hurt on defense in this case because we were using a 1-3-1 zone defense at the time. By the way, we won the tournament that year and this move really helped us to win that championship.

We never run this set for an entire game. A good idea is to start the first and second halves with it. If a coach doesn't really plan to use it much during a game, he should run it just before the half. The other team usually spends the entire half-time making adjustments and forgetting about the other offensive sets. In the second half, a team can go back to their regular offense. Thus, you not only confuse their half-time talk or cause them to waste a timeout, but you get a chance to have some fun at someone else's expense.

BLENDING IN THE PICKS-AND-SCREENS FROM THE LOW POST

We like the low post plays, so we decided to run as many of them off the high post as we could. We had to make sure that the guards were not duplicating their cuts so that the rest of the players could know what was going on. Figure 3-14 shows some of the moves we like, namely "The Double Screen Guard in the Corner" and the guard special plays. The center and G^2 see that G^1 is going straight down the free throw lane, so they understand that the scissor or "Double Screen on the Forward" play is not on.

Guards' Double Screen in Corner

Player G^1 on this play goes straight down toward the baseline. Player G^2 is always geared to start the scissors play when G^1 passes to F^1. Player G^2 has plenty of time to adjust his move as the low post plays develop. The center follows his rule of watching G^1, so that as G^1 goes toward the baseline, the center moves to that side to become part of the low post plays (Diagram 3-14).

Player G^1 then makes his move to the corner and G^2 pulls up and makes room for G^1 coming out of the corner.

Guard Special—Option I (or) Center Pop

Player G^1 passes to F^1 and heads straight down to the baseline. Player G^2 and the center start their moves when G^1 pulls up deep; the team knows that the guard special is on (Diagram 3-14). As in the low post, the center has the option of posting or popping out for the ball, as was explained in Chapter 2.

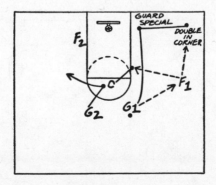

Diagram 3-14

Forward Special

As G^1 dribbles at F^1, F^1 will move toward the free throw lane. The center pops out to the guard position and the play is run exactly like the low post forward special with all its options.

Pick-and-Post

Instead of F^1 using a V-cut to receive a pass from G^1, he comes right up and sets a belly-up screen on the man guarding G^1. The guard sets his man up with a fake and picks him off the screen and looks for a shot. If there is a switch, he has the option of getting the ball to F^1 on a "Roll and Post," as shown in Diagram 3-15. If F^1 is much taller then the guard who switched on him, F^1 has the option of calling out "Fish." The rest of the team spreads out, as was discussed in Chapter 1.

If the defense is giving a lot of back-side help, then it would be wise to go the "Double High Post," because this eliminates any kind of help on the "Pick-and-Post." The forwards have the option of screening directly for the guards on any set. If the forward chooses not to, then he does a V-cut to receive the ball.

Over the Top

This play is easily adjusted to our high post. The play is always set up by the guard passing to the forward and going

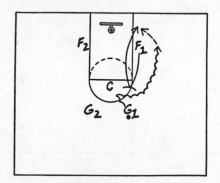

Diagram 3-15

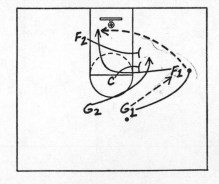

Diagram 3-16

over to him to get the ball back. The center moves over to set a spot screen just below the free throw line and F^2 follows his rule of filling in high or low depending where the center screens (Diagram 3-16).

Player G^2 waits until G^1 receives the ball back from F^1 and then he scissors a little wider than the original high post scissor play.

SUMMARY

In the last two chapters, the basic plays were run off two different sets.

Coaches talk a great deal about movement without the ball. We don't believe in having a player running around just trying to keep busy. Player F^2, for instance, knows he is a rebounder in the high post when G^1 has the ball. He is also aware that if G^1 passes to F^1 he might be set up for a shot off a twin screen.

This is our version of movement without the ball. This system gives each player a specific place to be, which helps a coach to be able to coach a player as to where he should be on the floor.

Rather than simply telling a player to "move" (which might be like telling a coach to control a chicken with its head cut off), a coach can tell a player where he should be and what he should be doing. This in turn allows you to teach a player to perform within a pattern so that he can learn to play his position in a game situation where events happen too quickly for a coach to suddenly direct the action. Furthermore, our pattern is not a predictable, monotonous one—the Pick-and-Screen has many built-in options where a team can free lance within a definite, defined pattern. Thus this offense has the advantage of being both a patterned and a free lance offense at the same time.

Finally, this offense keeps the players' minds on the game and at all times gives each player the excellent rebounding position that is so important at any level of the game.

4

ORGANIZING THE SIDE POST PICKS AND SCREENS

The side post is a special set for us. We use it sparingly during the season, but we will go to it when we want to jam the ball deep as quickly as possible. Our secondary purpose would be to create a mismatch ("Fish"). When we use this set, our team knows that we have one thing in mind—getting the ball inside.

We would like the guard who handles the ball to have the smallest man guarding him. We also like our strongest inside player to be away from the ball. In Diagram 4-1, F^2 is the strongest inside player and G^1 has the smallest guard covering him. Note in Diagram 4-1 that all the players are lined up in the low post set, except for the center. The center lines up so he favors one side of the free throw lane and stands just above the free throw line. In this position, the defensive center has to move up to cover the center and this opens up the area near the basket.

Most teams have their big men screen for each other in the deep positions. We like to screen for a big man by using our guard as a screener. In this way, if the defensive men switch, a team has something extra going for them; namely, a mismatch.

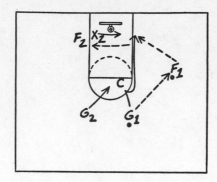

Diagram 4-1

This set gives the players an awareness of constantly moving inside with the ball. We like to use this set late in a game when we need a basket or a possible three-point play.

PICK OFF THE CENTER
(Diagram 4-1)

Although we want to go deep, the first option is the guard picking his man off the center's spot screen. If G^1 is open, F^1 will pass him the ball. If there is back-side help, G^1 will feed the ball to F^2 on the other side of the basket.

SCREEN OPPOSITE BIG MEN
(Diagram 4-2)

If G^1 doesn't get the ball, he pulls up deep as if he was setting up the low post guard special. He pauses for one count and then goes across the lane and uses a belly-up screen on the defensive man guarding F^2. When G^1 passed to F^1 and G^1 made his cut, G^2 was driving his man deep behind the center and breaking out by picking his man off the center.

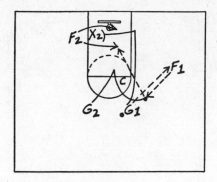

Diagram 4-2

If G^1 does not get the ball and F^1 passes back to G^2, G^1 then sets his screen so that F^2 can either go below or over the top of G^1's belly-up screen. When F^2 clears the basket, G^2 jams the ball into him for a deep power shot.

POP THE GUARD
(Diagram 4-3)

When the ball is being passed to G^2, the center counts to two and releases deep to pin screen for G^1, who pops out to the free throw line. If G^2 cannot get the ball into F^1, G^2 looks for G^1 popping out. This move prevents the defensive man on G^1 from doubling up on F^2.

The center must use a "radar" screen on G^1's man. This means that he does not just go to a spot to screen, but seeks out the defensive man and runs right at him to pin him down.

If the center goes down to screen and sees that F^2 is receiving the ball, he moves to a rebounding position away from the shot.

If G^2 passes the ball to G^1 as he pops out, G^1 will look to shoot. If the shot is not there, he will look for the center, who has made a quick post after he screened for G^1. If neither option is there, G^1 can either go back-side with a screen from the center or reset the offense.

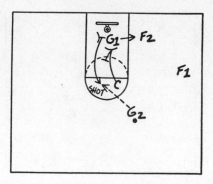

Diagram 4-3

Some teams like to sag, so when G^2 has the ball and tries to jam it into F^2, G^2 has the option of passing back to F^1. Player F^1 must look for a shot or a drive so that he is a threat. This will keep the defensive man tight on F^1 and open up the lane for a pass to F^2.

If F^1 finds that the man guarding him is taking away G^2's passing lane to F^2 by his sagging in, then F^1 has the option of passing directly to F^2 rather than to G^2.

We like to send the guard (who has the smallest man guarding him) down to screen for F^2 for obvious reasons. When the guard goes across the free throw lane to screen for F^2 and the defense switches, there is a built-in mismatch. We couldn't ask for anything better because this fits in perfectly with our mismatch game.

OPEN SIDE OFFENSE

If we are in the side post set and G^2 has the ball but cannot pass to G^1, he has the option of executing the open side offense as discussed in Chapter 2. The center is the only player who has to make any adjustments if he is involved in any open side plays.

If G^2 wants to play two-on-two basketball with F^2, he waves off the center with his hand as he comes down the court. This tells the center not to adjust to the open side but to stay at the side post position.

BLENDING IN THE LOW POST PLAYS

We had to make a decision whether to set the center in the side post position or just have him come up higher than usual on the low post set. We decided that the side post would be more effective for the following reasons:

1. It allows a better angle for G^1 to pick his man off the center for a lay-up.
2. It blends in with the low post guard special look, but this time the guard concentrates on screening for the opposite big man.
3. It alerts F^2 that he is the main target and allows him to set his man up accordingly.
4. It forces the defense to play closer on the center because of the threat of him receiving a pass and shooting. This opens up the deep passing lane for F^2.

If G^1 has the ball and wants to blend in the low post plays, he passes to F^1 and cuts behind the center, instead of ball side. This move alerts the rest of the players that G^1 is setting up the guard special or he might go to the corner to set himself up for the "Double Screen in the Corner" play.

Player G^1 could also dribble right at F^1 to set up the forward special. He can pass to F^1 and follow his pass to set up the "over-the-top" play. The peek play could be run off this set, but we don't want F^2 moving up to the free throw line. We are trying to get the ball into F^2 in the deep position and we don't want him moving around too much. However, if we were strictly a side post team, we would definitely blend the peek series into this set.

The high post plays could be used with this set by bringing the ball down the outside one-third of the court, as shown in Diagram 4-4. This would signal that the high post plays are being set up. We prefer to stay away from the high post plays because we don't like the guards scissoring outside of the free throw lane. Another reason is our desire to remain within our philosophy of never having the guards dribbling too close to the sidelines. That is the reason we always line up our guards on the free throw boundary lines extended. We have learned

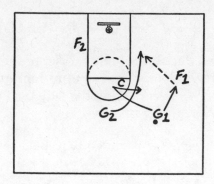

Diagram 4-4

that by having the guards in this position we are able to get a better passing angle to the forwards. If the guard is too near to the sideline, this position makes the defensive forwards' job very simple, because the defensive player can more easily overplay the forward and not have to worry so much about a difficult adjustment to a back door pass.

Remember that although this set is in our playbook, we don't always need to use it. If we didn't have a strong big man (one who can power dribble), we would not put this part of the offense in during the season.

SUMMARY

By moving the center around, a team creates a different look for the defense. This movement also signals some special plays that we want to use. In the side post set we want to go deep for a possible power move to the basket or to create a "Fish."

Although we have different sets, we basically do the same thing all the time. The next chapter shows a set that spreads out the defense so that the ball can be fed to either of the two deep post men. It is considered our inside attack.

5

UTILIZING PICKS AND SCREENS FOR THE INSIDE ATTACK (32-SET)

The main theory of this offense is to get the ball into the deep post men. If a team has one or more players who have the knack of taking that first big drop step to the basket, this would be the set to use. A team could get the same results with the low and high post sets, but this set spreads the offense out a little more and allows the post men more room to make their moves. This set also keeps the defense from doubling up on any one player.

This set is referred to as an inside offense because its main purpose is to get the ball inside. What makes it such a strong attack is that we found a way to blend this inside game with the low post plays which are so effective.

Diagram 5-5 depicts the lineup to start the 32 offense. The coach has to make a decision on where certain players should play. In Diagram 5-1, we made the decision that F^2 and the center were the best post men. We also decided that G^2 and F^1 were more effective as outside shooters, while G^1 was a good ballhandler and could still score from the outside or penetrate inside for a shot or a pass off.

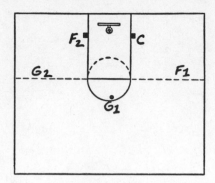

Diagram 5-1

The 32 set is more effective if the best outside shooter is on the same side of the basket as the best post man. Thus, if the defense sags off to help on the post man, then the outside shooter becomes an effective threat.

To keep the illustrations simple, we will leave G^2 and F^1 in the positions that they are shown in Diagram 5-1. To get to these positions, they could use V-cuts or interchange positions with F^2 and the center. When G^1 is in position to start the offense, F^2 and the center can go down and screen so that G^2 and F^1 can reach the wing positions by picking off the screens.

FEED THE POST MAN

Because there is a lot of posting in the Pick-and-Screen system, we spent a good amount of time with drills that are designed to get the ball inside. These drills and the actual techniques of posting are discussed in Chapters 11 and 10 respectively.

Every coach knows that good teams will work exceptionally hard to deny the ball to a post man, and that good teams get help from the perimeter players. If a team is not working hard, all a team has to do is pass the ball to F^2 or the center and let them make their different posting moves.

It is apparent that the offense must help to compensate for weakside help, ball side perimeter help, and for an individual defensive player guarding the post man by taking away the passing angle to the post.

Clear the Back Side (Diagrams 5-2, 5-3)

If G^1 passes the ball to F^1 and F^2 sees the defensive man fronting or playing halfway in front on the low side of the center, F^2 will break toward F^1. This move opens up the back side so that F^1 can pass over the top ("alley-oop") to the center (Diagram 5-2).

If the defensive man is playing halfway in front of the center on the high side, F^2 will clear the area by moving along the baseline side as shown in Diagram 5-3.

Player F^1 has the option of passing the ball to F^2 as he comes to the ball side. If F^2 receives the ball he can shoot (if not being pressured) or he can feed the center. Either way, F^2's move takes away the back-side help that most teams use to stop the deep pass.

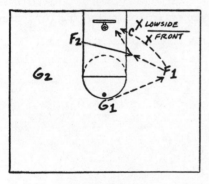 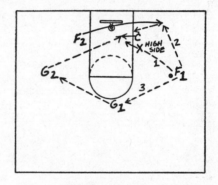

Diagram 5-2   Diagram 5-3

Reverse the Ball

If F^1 has the ball and sees the defensive man fronting or halfway in front of the center, then F^1 has three passing options: (1) feed the center; (2) pass the ball to F^2, who is clearing the back side; (3) reverse the ball back to G^1, as shown in Diagram 5-3.

If G^1 gets the ball, he looks immediately for the center and passes to him if he has good position. The ball can actually be reversed all the way to G^2 if necessary to create what we call a passing angle to the center.

The reverse move puts a lot of pressure on the defense. One moment the defensive man has good position to stop the initial pass to the center and the next move he finds himself trailing the center as the ball is reversed.

Screen Back Side (Diagram 5-4)

Player F^2 and the center can screen for each other across the lane any time they feel that they aren't getting good post-up positions by staying on one side of the basket. This move will create openings underneath and a possible switch that might result in a poor defensive player picking up a stronger post man.

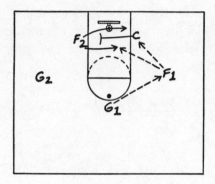

Diagram 5-4

OUTSIDE SCREEN—QUICK POST (Diagram 5-5)

This is still another reason we want the best shooter on the same side of the basket as the strongest post man. Besides its keeping the defense from sagging, it also gives the players a chance to play two-on-two basketball on that side of the court. The outside screen is used to free the good shooter for a shot and to work for a possible "Fish" in a pick-and-post situation. Diagram 5-5 depicts the outside screen that results in a pick and post. If the shot is not there and G^2 is looking for F^2 posting, then all the options used in feeding F^2 directly, over the top or reversing the ball are employed.

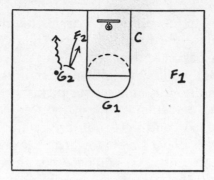

Diagram 5-5

SCISSOR PICK (Diagram 5-6)

The first rule of the scissor pick is that the player who passes cuts first. This rule takes care of any doubts on who should be first. Another rule is that the second cutter should receive the ball. This eliminates a lot of turnovers at the point of exchange.

When G^1 has the ball and he can't pass to the wings, either F^2 or the center can break up to the corner of the free throw line. If both of them break up and the ball is passed to center, then F^2 would fade back to his original position.

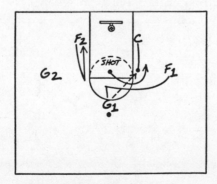

Diagram 5-6

If G¹ passes to the center, G¹ drives his man toward the baseline then cuts tight to the center. While G¹ is cutting, F¹ steps toward the basket and comes around the center. Player F¹ picks his man off G¹ and again (if needed) off the center as the center gives him the ball. This scissor pick should end up with F¹ getting a good percentage shot in the free throw circle.

If G¹ passes to F¹ and the center breaks up, F¹ can pass the ball to the center. F¹ will step towards the basket and then scissor around the center. G¹ will become the second cutter by stepping towards the basket and coming around the center while picking his man off F¹. Player G¹ will either end up with a jump shot or a drive to the basket.

BLENDING IN THE LOW POST PLAYS

Peek Play (Diagram 5-7)

If the defense is denying the pass from G¹ to G², then F² will break up to the corner of the free throw line and receive a pass from G¹. Player G² can either work the scissor play or peek to the basket. If G² does not receive the ball from F², G² continues his move and screens for F¹ on the other side of the basket. Note that in Diagram 5-7, G² is screening at two different positions. He is applying a radar screen (seeking out the path of the defender), so he is looking for the defender coming above or below the center's back-on screen.

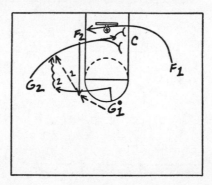

Diagram 5-7

After G^1 passes to F^2, G^1 drives his man down to the free throw line, then cuts in front of F^2 looking for a return pass. If G^1 receives the ball from F^2, he has the options of shooting, driving to the basket or passing to F^1 in the deep position. All the other options off the peek play are the same as discussed in Chapter 2.

Also, if the defense is denying the pass from G^1 to G^2, G^2 can screen F^2's man in such a manner that G^2 is now in the low post and F^2 becomes the wing. You have the advantage to this exchange if you have a physically strong guard or a guard with good individual inside moves. The guard may be able to take advantage of a mismatch inside. This exchange is also advantageous if F^2 is a good passer, shooter, or driver. He may utilize his skills by drawing a less agile defensive forward outside with him.

Pop the Wing (Diagram 5-8)

By raising his right or left hand over his head, G^1 gives the signal to pop one of the wings around a twin screen. When he raises his right hand (closed fist), F^1 will head toward the basket with the thought of picking his man off the center and then continuing on to use the twin (belly-up) screen set by F^2 and G^2. Player G^2 will actually use a radar screen looking for the man guarding F^1 coming over the top or below F^2's screen. Player G^1 will keep the ball alive until F^1 gets to his position and then passes him the ball. A good way for G^1 to help this

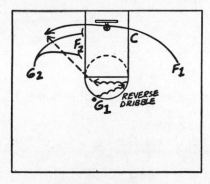

Diagram 5-8

timing is to dribble toward the opposite corner of the lane and then reverse dribble to his original spot in order to hit F¹ coming around the double screen. This play is a takeoff of the guard pop in the peek series from Chapter 2.

Guard Special and the Double Screen Guard in Corner (Diagram 5-9)

Player G^1 passes the ball to F^1 and cuts to the basket. The center moves up when G^1 cuts and is ready to receive the ball from F^1 to set up the guard special. As soon as G^1 pulls up deep (which is the key to run the play), F^1 will pass to the center and run right at G^1. This play and all its options were discussed in detail in Chapter 2.

If G^1 decides to go to the corner, then F^1 will pass the ball to G^1 and F^1 will screen for G^1. As G^1 dribbles out of the corner, the center sets up the second part of the tandem screen. This play was also diagrammed and discussed in Chapter 2.

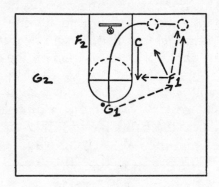

Diagram 5-9

Forward Special—Center Pop (Diagram 5-10)

Player G^1 dribbles right at F^1 setting up the forward special. Player F^1 heads for the basket and quickly pivots to get into a post position. If G^1 cannot pass the ball to F^1, then the center pops out to a guard position and G^1 passes to him and runs right at F^1. Player F^1 will then run away from G^1 until he is on the other side of the basket. When F^1 clears the basket he will change direction and use G^1's screen, looking for a pass from the center. All the options of the forward special were illustrated in Chapter 2.

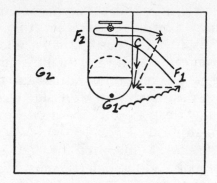

Diagram 5-10

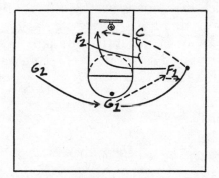

Diagram 5-11

Over-the-Top Pick (Diagram 5-11)

Player G^1 passes to F^1 and goes over to F^1 to receive a return pass. Player F^2 follows the rule of filling in the high or low position depending on where the center is playing. Player G^2 will move over to the top of the key and has the option of scissoring around F^2 and the center or just staying at the top of the key (which will replace G^1's spot on the floor).

Player F^1 hands the ball back to G^1 and picks his man off F^2. Player G^1 then passes the ball over the top to F^1. The options used are similar to those discussed in Chapters 2 and 3.

SUMMARY

Although we use some of our basic low post perimeter plays in this set, we still consider this set an inside attack. The inside game is very important to any offense. It is a truism that an overpowering inside game has the most effect on offensive success. If a team can post up tough and complement it with their perimeter game, they will be successful. If we don't have anyone who can post tough, then we stay away from this set and work the ball deep by running a peek series or double screen off the high post.

We don't do a lot of different things in this set, but it does give us another look and the defense must adjust to this new look. Often a defense may stop one of our sets temporarily. Our complementary set will present an entirely different set of problems, which then opens up the offense. By switching sets back and forth during a game, we stay aggressive on offense and keep the defense constantly off guard. Again we seem to have a lot of plays and sets, but we execute one or two special moves off each set with all the basic plays blending in very smoothly.

6

COACHING THE PICK-AND-SCREEN AGAINST SPECIAL HALF-COURT DEFENSES

PRESSURE (MAN-TO-MAN)

We never want a defense dictating to us what we are going to do offensively. At all times we want to run our normal set plays. To accomplish this against half-court pressure we move our sets up proportionately to the pressure. Diagram 6-1 depicts the low post set when the pressure is at midcourt. The players are coached where to line up, rather than just telling them to move up proportionately to the pressure. With the players in the position shown in Diagram 6-1, the low post plays are ready to be executed.

The Low Post

It is crucially important that our guard keep his dribble so that he cannot be trapped and so that he has the option of driving. We want the guard passing off the dribble.

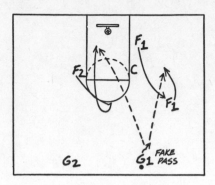

Diagram 6-1

The first thing we want to do is take advantage of the pressure on the forward as he breaks out to receive the ball in the wing position. If F^1 breaks toward the sideline and is being denied the pass from G^1, he is coached to show a closed fist with his target hand. This is the signal for G^1 to fake the pass and F^1 will then break back toward the basket setting up a back door move as shown in Diagram 6-1.

This type of move can also be used by F^2 as he breaks up to the top of the key to start the peek play series. If F^2 breaks up toward the ball and is being denied the pass from G^1, F^2 will straighten out his right arm and show a closed fist. Player G^1 will fake the pass to F^2 and then F^2 will break to the basket (Diagram 6-1).

The peek series off the low post is an excellent offense to use against pressure defenses. This series has some moves that are just made for this type of defense. If F^2 breaks up to the top of the key and receives a pass from G^1, F^2 looks for G^2 breaking to the basket (Diagram 6-2). If G^2 is not open, F^2 looks for G^1 coming across in front of him. At this time the center is moving toward the baseline while F^1 starts his move to the basket. All the options of the peek series that were discussed in Chapter 2 are now triggered.

We feel that our picks are even more effective if the defense is guarding us closely. Besides the give-and-go situations that can be used along with the back doors, the players actually have more room near the basket (after their picks) to make their individual shooting moves.

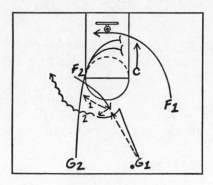

Diagram 6-2

In this offense you don't necessarily have to pass the ball to get a series started. Therefore, if teams are denying the initial passes, the guard can dribble to get the same results. When F^2 breaks up to the top of the key for the peek series, G^1 can drive his man down with the dribble and cut across in front of F^2 and pick his man off.

Player G^1 could also dribble right at F^1 in the wing position if he wants to set up the forward special. All these options are illustrated in Chapter 2.

The High Post

This set is easily adapted to half-court pressure. Again, the players move up to their new positions in proportion to the pressure. Diagram 6-3 shows a scissor play and a possible dou-

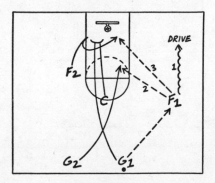

Diagram 6-3

ble screen. Note that F^2 is working his way toward the basket before he breaks over the top. This move allows F^2 to get a better picking angle, and he is also getting a closer shot at the basket.

All the plays that are illustrated in Chapter 3 can be run against this type of pressure. The low post plays can also be blended in with the high post set as shown in Chapter 3.

Double High Post (Diagram 6-4)

The first option is to take advantage of the overplaying of the defensive men on F^1, F^2, and the center. If the defense is denying the pass to any one of the three, we want them to show the closed fist. The guard will then fake a pass to that man and that player will break to the basket.

The advantage the double high post has over the normal high post is the spreading out of the defense to a point where they cannot double up or give any back-side help. If any player ever gets by their man on a back door, a scissor play, or a one-on-one drive to the basket, there is no way the defense can recover to help on that man.

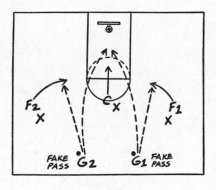

Diagram 6-4

PICK-AND-SCREEN AGAINST THE SAGGING MAN-TO-MAN

We are a shooting team, so very few teams sag against us. It brings to mind two particular games. One was a regional game and another was a first round state tournament game. In both cases, the defense decided to sag. None of their players were above the free throw line. We didn't do anything special, just went to the first option, and that is to shoot. The scores at the halves were 43-13 and 45-15. The only thing we could figure out was that their scouting reports indicated that if they stopped our deep Picks-and-Screens they could stop our attack. The obvious question would be, "What if you're not hitting from the perimeter?" Remember, that we consider our offense a "shoot and storm the board attack."

We treat rebounding as an extension to the offense. In Chapter 8 the rebounding techniques will be discussed and it will show how we use rebounding as part of the offense. If we are not hitting from the outside and a team is sagging, we are confident that our soft shot will result in a good rebounding ball. Our shooters feel that their missed shots are passes coming off the rim.

If we try to go deep and the defense is sagging, we like to go back side in a hurry and quick pick off that side as shown in Diagram 6-5.

Other moves that work well against the sagging man to man are:

1. Double screen guard in corner
2. Guard special
3. Pop the guard (off the peek play)

We prefer, however, to keep running the back-side offense to one side and then to the other until something opens

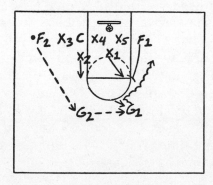

Diagram 6-5

up. We are willing to take the 15-to-20 ft. shot, so sagging doesn't bother us. Because of the movement of the forwards in the deep position and the deep picks, teams don't sag on us. We find that when using this offense, teams will use weakside help rather than attempting to sag.

PICK-AND-SCREEN VERSUS
THE WEAKSIDE HELP DEFENSES

Opponents will try to use weakside help to take away the deep picks away from the ball. Some defenses will not follow the screener across the lane, but will stay on the ball side of the lane to plug up the deep shooting positions. As a result we have used a lot of guard, forward and center pops to counter this type of strategy. We have discussed this type of move in Chapters 2 and 3. We also found that the back-side offense is suitable for this type of defense. By popping around the guards and forwards during the course of a game, the opponents will lose the effectiveness of their weakside help and in some cases will even abandon it altogether.

If we are playing a team that is quick enough to use weak-side help and can still recover to stop the quick back-side moves or the pops, then we will set up the double high post. This set will neutralize any weakside help.

Pick-and-Post Versus Pick-and-Roll

In the previous chapters we have been using the words Pick-and-Post rather than the traditional Pick-and-Roll. There is a definite reason for this. When we first started using the Pick-and-Screen attack, we would always roll to the basket. Over a period of time we noticed a drop in the guards' shooting percentages. We came to the conclusion that the guards were not applying their first rule of the Pick-and-Screen, and that is to shoot. They were either looking to the roll for their first option or in some cases had the roll and shooting on their minds at the same time. When we eliminated the roll option, the guards' percentages increased.

Another reason we went to the post rather than the roll was the weakside defenses that came into the picture. In order for the roll to be effective, the man rolling has to be heading directly toward the basket. This results in either a stolen pass or a possible charging foul (Diagram 6-6).

With the Pick-and-Post, the man screening does a roll toward the baseline, outside of the free throw lane, and will then post up. The guard picks off the screen and looks to shoot or drives for the basket. If the shot is not there, he pulls back with the idea to look for the screener who is posting. If there is a switch on the screen, we have created a "Fish," which is what we want in our mismatch game.

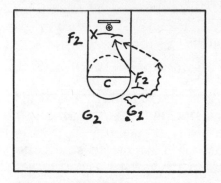
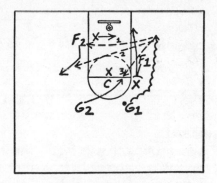

Diagram 6-6   **Diagram 6-7**

In order for the weakside help to be effective, the defensive man would have to come all the way across the lane and this would result in F^2 being open underneath for a pass across the lane (Diagram 6-7). Player F^2 could also move away from the lane to create an even greater distance between the defensive man X and himself, as shown in Diagram 6-7. This forces the defense to cover more area. The ball could also be reversed to the back side for a back-side pick. Player F^2 could also pop out to the free throw area for a medium-range shot, as is illustrated in Diagram 6-8. We believe that we can move the ball faster than the defense can move, so F^2 should be open for a shot.

Still another reason we use the post rather than the roll is the feeling that a good defensive team will not give you the roll.

When you are stressing good defense in your own practices, it's almost impossible to practice the roll, so we just stay with the Screen-and-Post.

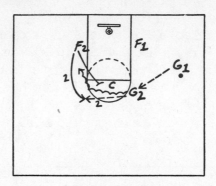

Diagram 6-8

THE TANDEM VERSUS THE HALF-COURT ZONE PRESSES (Diagram 6-9)

When our offense reads the half-court defense to be a zone defense, we go right into the tandem attack. This is the only set we use against any type of midcourt zones. In the tandem attack we are not necessarily trying to score an easy basket. We try to work the ball into a position that forces the defense to move back far enough in the front court for us to determine whether they plan to stay in a zone or if they are going to switch to a man-to-man defense. Diagram 6-9 shows the players in the tandem set against a 1-3-1 trap defense.

Player G^1 dribbles the ball up to midcourt, but doesn't cross the midcourt line. When he gets to the midcourt line, F^1 will break toward the sideline behind the defensive man on that side. Player F^2 will step forward, looking for the pass from G^1. If the pass is not there, G^1 will pass to G^2 in the backcourt, as shown in Diagram 6-10. F^2 will then break toward the sideline behind the defensive man on his side while F^1 moves back to the middle of the court. Although we prefer the ball being passed to the middle of the court, the guards have the option of passing the ball to either F^1 or F^2 as they move back and forth from the middle to the sideline.

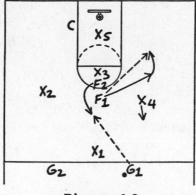

Diagram 6-9

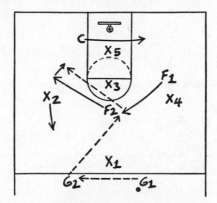

Diagram 6-10

You will find out that the guards can pass the ball back and forth at least three times in the backcourt before using up their 10 seconds. By this time, one of the forwards will be open. The guard also has the option of dribbling across the midcourt line if he feels that the defense is far enough back so that the defense cannot trap him before he has time to make his initial pass.

Having the forwards break behind the defensive forwards causes the defense to move back to cut them off, allowing the guards to take the ball into the front court. If the defense doesn't move back, then the ball can be passed to the forward breaking to the sideline. The number one option, however, is to get the ball to the middle if at all possible. Diagram 6-10 illustrates the movement after the pass is made from one guard to the other. It also shows the options that formulate once the middle man has the ball. The center will line up on the side away from the ball. As the ball is passed from G^1 to G^2, the center moves to the other side of the lane. This helps to set up a two-on-one break. If we don't get the two-on-one break, we will set up according to what the defense is playing.

No matter what kind of midcourt zone pressure we face, we have the tandem men set up at the top semicircle of the free throw lane as shown in Diagram 6-9.

THE DEEP PASS CHALLENGES A DOUBLE-UP DEFENSE

In the last few years, defenses have been trying to throw the Pick-and-Screen offense off its timing by doubling on the guards at half court, as shown in Diagram 6-11.

To counter this, we put into our playbook a deep pass to the basket. Diagram 6-11 illustrates the double-up play. It is a simple move, but very effective. We consider a double-up to be two defensive guards doubling on one of the guards. When this occurs, the whole team hollers, "Double-up," and the guard with the ball looks for the deep pass. The importance of communication on the court by players cannot be over-emphasized.

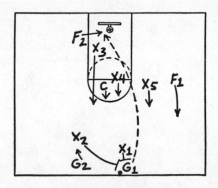

Diagram 6-11

No matter what set we are in when the double-up occurs, the center will move up to the top of the key to open up the area under the basket.

The forward on the side of the ball will also move up, forcing his man to move up with him. When G^1 hears the "double-up" call, he does a quick read of the defense. If the defense is rotating their defensive forward up to cover G^2, then G^1 passes the ball to F^2. If the forward doesn't rotate up, then the pass will be either to G^2 or the center. If G^2 gets the ball he will be able to move in for a medium-range shot or drive until someone picks him up, passing off to the open man.

SUMMARY

We feel that the offense becomes even more effective when opponents pressure us at midcourt. It opens up more driving lanes and it is easier to screen and pick a man off who is playing tight on the offensive man with the ball. If the pressure is farther out than half court, we treat it as full-court pressure and get the entire team involved in some unique plays to neutralize the full-court pressure. The full-court attack will be discussed in Chapter 9.

By staying with the Screen-and-Post rather than Screen-and-Roll, our shooting percentage has increased considerably. We attribute this to the players' habit of looking for the shot rather than the roll after a pick. Our own defense doesn't give any team the roll, so it is easier to practice the post move rather than the roll. With all the different types of zones and weakside help defenses being used against us, we feel that posting fits better into the Pick-and-Screen offense. Now we have more time to concentrate on one move in practice, and that move is the Screen-and-Post.

7

ATTACKING ZONES
WITH THE PICK-AND-SCREEN

Through the years, opponents have used a variety of zone defenses to stop the Picks-and-Screens used in our system. We like to see zones played against us because we do spend a lot of time in our practices posting and bringing the back-side players to the middle or baseline side following a screen. This prepares us for our man-to-man attack as well as for a zone attack. Our perimeter shooting becomes even more effective against a zone because we actually have more time and less pressure in getting our shots off.

We don't use the word "pick" in attacking zones as much as the word "screen." You can't actually pick a player off a screen while working the ball around the zone, but instead, we use the screen as a means of clearing a certain area for a good percentage shot.

We don't use a screen on every move we make against a zone, but when we do it is quite effective.

Most teams like to move the ball fast around a zone. We would rather pass the ball to one side of the zone and then make sure the zone has completely shifted in one direction.

This creates what we call blind spots in a zone defense. With the ball on one side of the court, the zone cannot see players flashing to the middle. Coming from behind the zone allows the ball to be passed to the middle, which in turn opens up a lot of opportunities for our offense. If the ball cannot be passed to the middle, then the ball is reversed quickly. This way, it takes longer for the defense to get into its proper positions and it is also forced to hustle more. Our method of zone offense creates passing lanes to the inside men as the zone is shifting over. Furthermore, there is more time to take a perimeter shot.

We always try to get the ball to the best perimeter shooters and coach them to take their shots with great concentration.

We've had a great amount of success against zones over the years and actually look forward to seeing one played against us.

---

32 SET—NORMAL

At times, we vary the attack against different zones, but we always consider ourselves in some kind of 32 set.

No matter which way we set the 32 offense, we always use some basic principles. We try to:

1. Force a defensive man to commit himself in order to open up a shooting area.
2. If possible, penetrate
   a. even-front defenses up the middle
   b. odd-front defenses down the free throw boundary line.
3. Send a man through the zone.
4. Use a reverse screen.
5. Create passing lanes with the movement of the ball.
6. Flash into the middle from behind the zone.
7. Go underneath the zone (baseline) when the ball is in the middle of the zone.
8. Make the defense adjust to stop our attack, then use special screens to counter what they are doing.
9. *Shoot* the medium-range shot.

We always put the best perimeter shooters in positions where they can take a shot the first time that they touch the ball. If the shot is not there, we counter with our different screens.

We identify the players in Diagram 7-1 as:

- B—Ball Handler
- 1—Best Perimeter Shooter
- 2—Second Best Perimeter Shooter
- R1—Best Rebounder
- R2—Second Best Rebounder

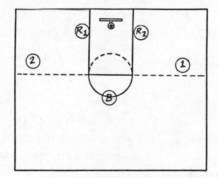

Diagram 7-1

Our statistical records and experience over the years have proven to us that a team can control more rebounds if the best rebounder is away from the shooter. Since 1 is the best shooter and is expected to take a good percentage of the perimeter shots, we want R1 to be the away rebounder.

If the defense is giving us more good shots in one area than another, we will interchange our players so that the attack will be more effective.

Players 1 and 2 place themselves below the free throw line extended. They are coached to stay in an area that is in their range of shooting. We stress this point because we want 1 and

2 to be able to shoot immediately upon receiving the ball if they are not overly pressured.

There are a lot of coaches who cringe when they hear this because they believe in passing a certain amount of times before they allow their teams to shoot.

The theory of shooting first and passing second against zones follows the offense philosophy of the Pick-and-Screen system.

Again, we used our findings from the many years of taking statistics as we have mentioned many times before.

The findings pointed out that teams—high school and colleges as well—will pass up the first good shot in order to pass the ball around the zone. What was the result? Once in a while they ended up with an opening in the zone for a lay-up or a short jump shot. But in most cases, the final shot would end up further away from the basket than the initial shot. Other shots were hurried under pressure, and some shots looked like the Peter Pan variety—a flying leap to the basket.

Our question to coaches is, "Why?" Why pass up a perfectly good percentage shot when you have good rebounding positions and your best shooter has the ball in his hands? After compiling our findings, it took us about ten seconds to decide that we would shoot the good shot right now and force the defense to put pressure on us.

Now when we watch games, we know that we made the right choice. We cringe every time we see a player pass up that first good shot for a lesser percentage shot.

We know that a lot of coaches like simplicity in breaking every zone by using one type of set. We feel that we can use our variety of sets to our advantage against any zone, especially, in our case, when we constantly lack height and strength in our players.

It is just a matter of playing our personnel in the right positions to take advantage of their best percentage shots. Because of our traditionally small teams, we have become a medium-range perimeter-shooting team with the idea of getting the ball inside to keep the defense honest.

32 SET AGAINST STANDARD ZONES

32 Set Versus the 2-3 Zone

We start out teaching the 32 zone attack by working against a 2-3 zone. As we face different zones we will be making adjustments or shifting the attack, but we are still in the basic 32 set.

Against the 2-3 zone, B tries to penetrate the middle to draw the defensive guards to him. If he can't penetrate, he passes to either 1 or 2. We would prefer that he pass to 1 if possible, considering that he is our best shooter as shown in Diagram 7-2. If B sees that the defensive forwards are cheating to the outside, he has the option of passing inside to either R^1 or R^2 as shown in Diagram 7-2.

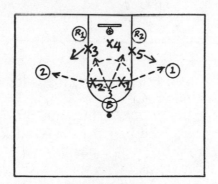

Diagram 7-2

When 1 has the ball, he looks to shoot and then looks for R^1 posting up. The players without the ball are instructed to always be looking for a lane opening in the middle of the zone. We refer to this move as "flashing through." Besides cutting through the front of a zone, we like to flash through from "behind" the zone. When 1 or 2 has the ball, the zone cannot see every offensive player, so we take advantage of this by flashing into the zone from the defense's blind side, as shown in Diagram 7-3.

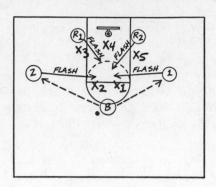

Diagram 7-3

The basic attack is keeping the ball moving around the zone until there is an open medium-range shot or a break in the middle of the zone. Most 2-3 zones have a tendency to favor one side of the court, so B is coached to pass away from the side the defense is leaning toward.

32 Cut Through Screen (Diagram 7-4)

If 1 has the ball and cannot pass the ball back to B or jam the ball into R[2] posting, R[2] breaks out to the short corner. Player 1 passes to R[2] and cuts through the zone. Player B moves over to receive the ball from R[2] and 2 rotates up to receive the pass from B. Then 2 passes to 1 for a short jump shot. Player R[1] takes up as much room as he can to put on a spot belly-up screen for 1 cutting through the zone. This pat-

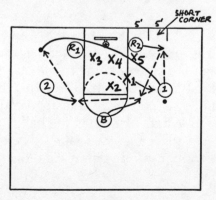

Diagram 7-4

tern achieves the goals of any zone offense: quick movement of the ball and the reverse of the ball. The unique feature is the screen for the shooter against the zone after the reverse.

If B cannot pass to 2, he passes over the zone directly to 1.

If R^2 breaks out to the side and 1 cannot pass him the ball or the ball is moving too slowly around the zone, 1 fakes the pass to R^2 and then passes back to B and 1 cuts through the zone. Player B then passes to 2, who is moving up, and 2 passes to 1 behind $R^{1\prime}$s screen.

32 Reverse-Screen (Diagram 7-5)

If we run the through pattern and the zone starts to shift quickly to deny the pass to 1, 2 will face the pass to 1 (who has already gone through) and pass back to B. Player R^1 sees the fake pass and goes across the lane and uses the spot belly-up screen set by R^2. Player 2 fakes the pass and passes back to B, who looks for R^1 coming around the screen.

We find that when we run the through pattern or reverse the ball, the defense will try to compensate and will forget to cut off R^1 or R^2 as the ball is moving. We instruct the man with the ball to be always looking for the openings in the seams of the zone for R^1 and R^2.

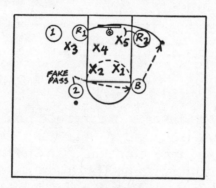

Diagram 7-5

32 Center Screen (Diagram 7-6)

If the defensive forward commits himself and is coming out to cover 1 or 2 when they have the ball, then we use R^1 or

R^2 as a screener on the defensive center. Player B tries to pene-trate the middle as he always does against a 2-3 zone, and bounce passes to 1. The bounce pass is the key for R^2 to screen the defensive center while R^1 comes around on the baseline side of the screen. We want 1 to shoot, but if the defensive forward is on him so quickly that he can't get the shot off, then we run this play or remind the players of this option during a time-out.

After R^2 screens the center, he will roll off and rebound away from the ball where R^1 came from. This restores the tri-angle rebounding positioning.

If nothing develops from this move, we are right back in the 32 set.

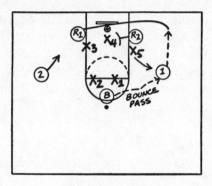

Diagram 7-6

32 Over Versus 1-3-1, 1-2-2, 3-2 Zones

We like to use this move against odd front defenses such as a 1-3-1, 3-2, or a 1-2-2 zone. We start out in the 32 normal set but this time B tries to penetrate the zone while dribbling down the free throw boundary line. This forces the defensive wing man (X^4) to pick him up. Then B will pass off the 1, who has moved down toward the baseline to get an open shot. Mean-while, 2 moves to the end of the free throw line inside of the circle (Diagram 7-7).

The first option for 1, after he receives the ball, is to shoot and then look for R^2 posting. Player 2 can flash through the

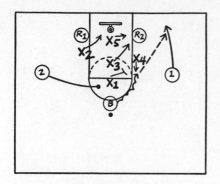 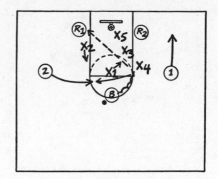

Diagram 7-7   Diagram 7-8

middle of the zone any time he sees an opening. Player R^2 is actually using a back-on screen (as he is posting), making it very difficult for X^5 to try and cover 1.

If the zone shifts over to take away the shot by 1, B will dribble toward X^4 and pass off to 2, as shown in Diagram 7-8. If B catches X^2 cheating up to steal the pass to 2, he will pass to R^1. Player 2 can either jam the ball to R^1 or give him an alley-oop pass (Diagram 7-8).

When 1 has the ball and cannot get off a good shot or pass to R^2 posting, he can pass back to B and run a through pattern as shown in Diagram 7-9. The reverse play with 2 faking the pass to R^1 and passing back to B while R^1 uses R^2's screen is also a possibility. We attack a 1-2-2 and a 3-2 zone exactly the same way as a 1-3-1, with B dribbling right at the defensive wing man.

It is worth mentioning again that we move our personnel around to take advantage of scouting reports or observations we make during a game. An example would be if X^2 was a great rebounder as illustrated in Diagram 7-8. We would move 1 on his side of the court so that X^2 would have to move away from the basket. We would also move R^1 on the opposite side of the basket away from the ball, which would give us even move rebounding strength.

Another change could take place between 1 and 2. If 2 is getting most of the shots but isn't hitting a good percentage, then 1 and 2 would change places in the offense.

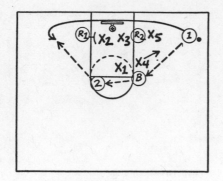 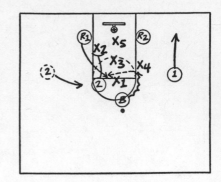

Diagram 7-9   **Diagram 7-10**

Weakside Screen (Diagram 7-10)

If a team is playing a 1-2-2 or a 1-3-1 zone and R^1 is a better than average shooter, we will set up the weakside screen.

As B dribbles at X^4, 2 screens X^2, allowing R^2 to come around the screen for a short jump shot. We use this screen when the defense is taking away the strongside attack and the ball is constantly being passed to 2. This screen is used as a changeup to prevent the defense from timing the pass to 2 and stealing the ball.

Rotation (Diagram 7-11)

When we call out, "Rotation," the players move right into the 32 over set. We want B to be lined up on the free throw boundary line extended and as high as the top of the free throw circle. At this position, he has good passing angles to 1 and 2. We don't want 2 facing B, but rather at a half turn toward the basket. This will allow him to shoot the ball as soon as he has it in his hands. Player 1 will line up below the free throw line extended in a position that's in his shooting range.

When the ball is passed to 1, 2 moves across the lane looking for a pass from 1. As 1 receives the ball, he looks to shoot. If he can't get the shot off, he looks for 2 in the middle of the zone, and if 2 cannot receive the pass, 1 will look for R^2 posting.

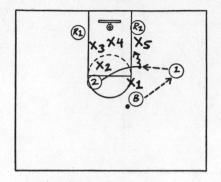 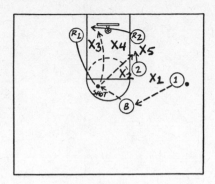

Diagram 7-11   **Diagram 7-12**

If 2 receives a pass from 1, he immediately turns toward the basket looking for the shot or a drive to the basket. If 2 draws X^4 toward him, he has the option of passing off to R^2, stepping underneath the zone toward the basket. Player 2 could also pass back to 1 if the defense sags in when he receives the initial pass. Then if 1 cannot get the shot off, and cannot pass the ball to 2 or R^2, he will pass the ball back to B. This usually happens if X^1 cheats over to cover 1 while X^2 picks up 2 cutting through the middle of the zone. This pass back to B triggers the following rotation. When the ball is in flight to B, R^1 rotates up to the corner of the free throw lane while R^2 crosses beneath the zone to the other side of the free throw lane. At this time, 2 moves down to fill the spot vacated by R^2 as shown in Diagram 7-12. Player B can now pass to R^1 (who is in a half turn to the basket position) or back to 1. If R^1 gets the pass, he looks to shoot. If the shot is not there, R^1 looks for R^2 underneath the zone or 2 on the opposite side of the basket.

If nothing develops, R^1 passes back to B and B passes to 1, starting the rotation all over again with R^1 moving across the lane toward 1.

Rotation Plus One (Diagram 7-13)

This move is a continuation of the rotation and is very effective. Player 2 rotates to his normal position as B passes to 1. However, this time 2 makes one more move using R^2 as a

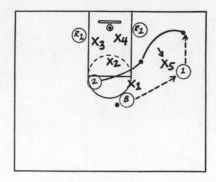

Diagram 7-13

screener. Player 2 uses this move if X^5 is moving out to cover 1. This is what we mean by making a defensive man commit himself. R^2 is always posting tough when 1 has the ball so the man guarding R^2 doesn't realize he is the one being screened. This gives 2 a chance to move into the short corner for a shot. (The normal rotation would still be on if 1 couldn't pass to 2 and the ball was passed back to B.) Player R^1 would still move up to the corner of the free throw lane while R^2 moves across the lane beneath the zone. Player 2 would move to the position that R^2 vacates. There is no special key for the man rotating through the zone and going to the short corner. He can use this move anytime he feels that he can get a shot from that area.

Reverse Rotation (Diagram 7-14)

This is a quick counter we use when the defense is following 2 through the rotation. Some defenses will only shift when 2 moves, which leaves a big gap in the defense. To take advantage of this, we use what we call a reverse rotation. We set up the reverse rotation during a timeout.

Player B will pass the ball to 1, but instead of 2 moving toward 1, R^2 rotates to that position. If R^2 receives the ball, he faces the basket and looks for a shot or drives. If these options are not available, R^2 looks for R^1 moving underneath the zone to the position that R^2 originally occupied. He can also look for 2, who moved down toward the baseline to take R^1's place. If nothing develops, the ball is passed to 1 or B and we continue on with the rotation options.

We keep running the reverse rotation until the defense takes it away from us, and then we go back to the normal rotation.

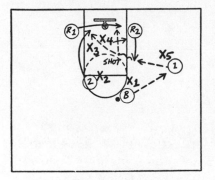
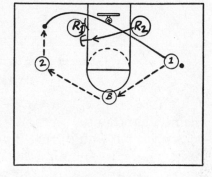

Diagram 7-14   **Diagram 7-15**

32 Double Screen (Diagram 7-15)

We call this the stack set. Player B passes the ball to 1 and, instead of R^2 posting, he fades away to the other side of the free throw lane. Player 1 passes back to B and goes through the zone using the twin screen set up by R^1 and R^2. The ball is then quickly reversed to 1 for a quick shot. This play is used mostly for a last second shot or any other situation when we want to get only one shot off.

PICK-AND-SCREEN AGAINST SPECIAL ZONES
(Diagram 7-16)

If the defense is using a box-and-one, diamond-and-one, or any other type of combination defense to stop our best shooter (1), we will then bring the word "pick" into the attack. If we feel that we must get 1 free in order to win a game, then we will add an extra screen or the basic through pattern. Diagram 7-16 depicts the extra screen by R^2 on the through pattern against a

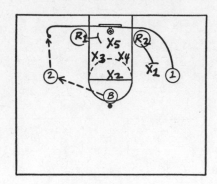

Diagram 7-16

diamond-and-one. If B cannot pass to 1, R^2 would still set the screen and 1 would pick his man off while 2 moves up to receive the pass from B. Player 1 uses the screen set by R^2 and then as he arrives at the other side of the basket, he picks his man (if needed) the second time off R^1's screen.

If you, as a coach, look at all the diagrams in this chapter, you can decide the best position for 1 to be at in order that a screen can be set for him. It could possibly be in the following: Diagrams 7-4, 7-9, 7-15, or 7-16.

If it was a deep man that the defense was trying to stop with a combination zone, and you needed that man to score in order to win, you could possibly use the following screens:

- Diagram 7-5 (reverse screen)
- Diagram 7-6 (screen directly on the defensive man guarding your best scorer instead of the center)
- Diagram 7-10 (weakside screen)

I must confess at this time, however, that through all my years of coaching there hasn't been a special type of zone played against my teams. We contribute this mostly to our multiple attack. It gives us the same balanced scoring we accomplish in our man-to-man offense. When you have this balanced scoring, there is no need for the defense to play a special zone.

SUMMARY

We've had a lot of success against zones over the years and actually look forward to having one used against us. We tell our players that if the opponent respects the job they are doing with the Pick-and-Screen offense, the only way they could possibly beat us is by using a zone. The opponent is actually paying our players a compliment by using a zone. Then our players go out and thank the other team by beating their zones. As a result, most teams, whether they start the game with a zone or are forced into it by all the picks and screens, usually get out of the zone in a hurry and then try some other method to beat us.

We refer to our zone offense as a multiple attack because we do so many different things with it. We are actually in an overload when we run the "Rotation Plus One" play. We're again in an overload when we use rotation. The attack is balanced until the defense uses an odd number front. Then we move the zone over to make a defensive man commit himself to open up a shooting area. The zone attack playbook has something for every type of talent your team could have. It takes away the fear that some teams have in facing a zone.

8

SETTING UP "THE BIG THREE" IN OFFENSIVE REBOUNDING

We have mentioned before that rebounding is as important to the Pick-and-Screen offense as shooting is. With good rebounding, our players are convinced that they can score every time they come down the court with the ball.

The first principle we stress in offensive rebounding is to rebound an area first, then look for a man to screen out in that area, and then get the ball.

In Diagram 8-1, we have lettered the rebounding positions as follows:

1. A is the rebounder away from the shot.
2. B is the ball-side rebounder.
3. M-F is the middle or is sometimes known as a floating rebounder.
4. G is the garbage man.
5. S is the safety man.

This is the way we want the players to rebound on every situation or play. We call this the "Big Three."

Diagram 8-1

1. The triangle formed by (A)—(B)—(M-F).
2. "The Garbage Pit" where (G) is rebounding.
3. The Safety Position where (S) is lined up.

This rebounding set came about through our many years of studying the bounce of the ball as it came off the rim. As we mentioned before, we had taken a *lot of statistics* to determine where most of the rebounds came off the rim or glass and who should be getting these rebounds.

THE TRIANGLE

Our first big finding was that teams were missing too many rebounds away from the shot because they just didn't fill this area. The away-from-the-shot position became the most important one in our offensive rebounding set. In fact, we don't even let any of our players shoot unless they know someone is ready to rebound in the "away" position. The exception, of course, would be if a player was shooting a lay-up. Our normal play patterns always take care of the away position, so the rule of not shooting applies, for the most part, on fast breaks or free lance situations.

We feel that if a player shoots and the ball comes off the rim to his side, he has a chance of getting his own rebound.

However, if it bounces to the away position and there is no one in that position, we have no chance at all to get the rebound. We like the highest possible percentage of getting every rebound that comes off the rim and therefore we want the away-from-the-shot area always covered.

The ball side (B) rebounding position is important, but it seems to be the easiest position to fill because most of the time, in any offense, a team has a man posting on ball side.

The middle rebounder does not always end up directly in front of the basket. He starts for that position, then looks for someone to screen out. This is executing the rule of area first, then a man in that area. In Diagram 8-1, you can see that we extended the middle position from one free throw boundary line to the other.

If the ball is shot and the middle rebounder is already close to the basket (Diagram 8-2), we coach him to step to the middle. We also gave the middle rebounder a second name of floater. In Diagram 8-3, F^1 has become a floating rebounder because G^1 has taken a shot. The ball side rebounder (the center) and F^2 are already in position. We don't want F^1 to run to the middle position, but rather gauge his speed under control and study the flight of the ball as he moves toward the middle position on the triangle. We have found out that he has a better chance of rebounding the ball if he floats toward the middle under control, rather than sprinting toward it.

In one of our championship years, we had a 5'10" forward

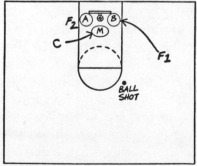

Diagram 8-2

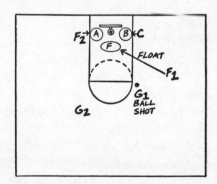

Diagram 8-3

by the name of Bob Blake. Because Bob was playing most of the year against 6'4" and 6'5" players, we tried to make sure that he ended up to be a floating rebounder, as much as possible, rather than stationing himself in the away or ball side positions. He was a strong player and ended up rebounding as if he were 6'4". This floating type of rebounding has become very important to the offense.

THE GARBAGE PIT

The garbage rebounder will position himself anywhere in the semicircle of the free throw lane (Diagrams 8-1 and 8-3). We call this the "garbage pit" because we have the players and especially the guards convinced that 70 percent of the rebounds come off toward the front of the basket than any other direction. The statistics show that not many rebounds come off deep to the sides, but more toward the front of the basket. The ball would have to clear the triangle before the garbage man would get the ball, so we consider a garbage rebound a bonus for us if we can get that type of rebound. Any ball that clears the triangle is considered a garbage rebound and we want it to result in a quick shot for two garbage points.

SAFETY

We try to keep the guards from rebounding in the triangle as much as possible. Instead, we would like them to be in the garbage or safety positions. That way, it is easier to get back into the offensive set a lot quicker, and this positioning keeps the bigger men in the high percentage rebounding positions.

The safety position is as close to the top of the key as possible (Diagram 8-1). We don't want the safety man too far out on the court so that, when we do rebound the ball and cannot put it right back up, he is in position to get back quickly into the offense. Another main concern is that when we are so wrapped up in running the offense, we don't want the other team getting a rebound and scoring easily on a fast break.

BASIC RULES OF THE "BIG THREE"

In this chapter, we will show how we apply our rules. Chapter 10 will discuss the techniques of rebounding, followed by the drills in Chapter 11.

Since we installed these basic rules and applied the insistance coaching technique to them, we have enjoyed many super years of rebounding. Looking back over our team statistics, we were only outrebounded by an average of three games a season and only one loss a year could be contributed to being outrebounded. This is not a bad statistic considering we are not noted for our tall players.

We aren't going to diagram every play we have and show the "Big Three" because such diagramming would be repetitious. We will go over certain plays and situations where we would apply the rules. This will be enough to show how we get consistent rebounding by the players on every shot.

The following rules are in the order of importance to our rebounding after a shot.

1. Fill position away from the shot.
2. Fill the safety position.
3. Fill the ball-side position.
4. Fill the middle position.
5. Fill the garbage position.

Guard's Rule

If one of the guards is farther away from the basket than the other guard when the ball is shot, the guard nearest to the basket has the garbage pit and the other guard goes to the safety position. If there is any doubt who is nearest, then they both go to the garbage pit. If the rebound comes off in the direction of one of the guards, that guard is considered the garbage man and the other guard goes to the safety position, as shown in Diagram 8-4.

If we are running a definite pattern, the position of the guards is predetermined. The guard rule, in relationship to the ball, was put in because of the free lancing situations that may occur while a play is being run.

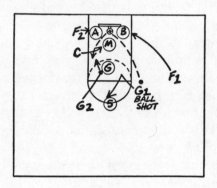

Diagram 8-4

Deep Man Rules

The deep men fill the triangle positions in the following order of importance:

1. Fill the away position.
2. Fill the ball-side position.
3. Fill the middle position.

The following rules were set up to help the deep men determine the positions they should fill in the triangle.

Rule #1

If two deep men are away from a shot, then the deepest man becomes the "away" rebounder and the other man is the middle rebounder (Diagram 8-4).

Rule #2

If a deep man is taking a shot immediately outside of the free throw lane, then Rule #1 applies as far as the deepest man goes. The other man will rebound the ball side. The shooter becomes the middle rebounder by floating to the position shown in Diagram 8-5.

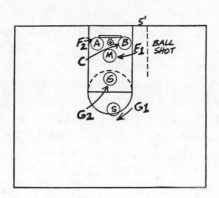

Diagram 8-5

We use this rule because we feel that if a player shoots from outside the free throw lane, he cannot get back to the ball-side position in time for the rebound. The defensive man has an inside position to start with and by the time the shooter comes down from his jump shot and tries to get to that position, the defense ends up with an advantage. It is easier for a player, after he shoots, to manuever around the defensive man with a fake and then float to the middle area. Again you could refer to this as "following your shot" where the shooter can watch the flight of the ball as he approaches the middle area for the rebound.

Rule #2a—Combo Rebounding

This rule is an extension of Rule #2. Combo means that two players work together in filling a certain rebounding area. In Rule #2, when the deep man took a shot immediately outside of the free throw lane, another man filled the ball side position and the shooter floated to the middle. Now we say in Rule 2a that if the shooter is taking a short corner or a corner shot as shown in Diagram 8-6, the guard furthest away from the shot will fill the middle and the forward will float to the garbage area. We feel that the guard furthest away has a better look at the ball and can study its flight as he moves to the middle. The short corner is approximately 5 feet to 10 feet from the free throw lane and a line tangent to the inside semicircle of the free throw lane. Any shot further than 10 feet from the lane we refer to as just a corner shot. In any of these two cases we apply the combo rule as illustrated in Diagram 8-6. If in doubt, the guard uses his own judgment. After working on this over and over again in practice, the guards are used to making the right judgment. If the guard is still in doubt, he applies the rule and the shooter will adjust himself to what the guard does as he steps in to rebound the middle or garbage. If we are constantly getting that type of situation in a particular game, it is very simple to make the adjustment from the bench by designating a particular player to fill the specific position.

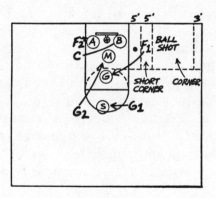

Diagram 8-6

Rule #3—Baseline Rebounding

We want the players that are going to end up in the away or ball-side positions in the triangle to head for the baseline first when they rebound. This prevents the triangle from looking like Diagram 8-7. We don't consider this a triangle. In all real-

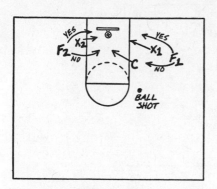

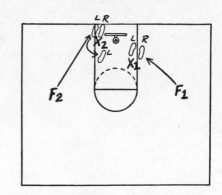

Diagram 8-7	Diagram 8-8

ity, Diagram 8-7 shows three middle rebounders. If we do end up as in the diagram, we find out that the players will rebound against each other.

We also find that the defense can control the rebounds that would bound out toward the sidelines. When we instilled the baseline rule, our rebounding improved immensely. We *insist* that the deep men go to the baseline side of the defensive man first and try to get their back side on the defensive man's hip. We don't expect the players to get between the man and the basket (unless he is playing against a careless opponent), but we do insist that the players wrap their legs around as F^1 is doing in Diagram 8-8.

If the defensive man is screening tough and takes a couple of more steps toward the baseline to screen out F^2 (Diagram 8-8), then F^2 will reverse pivot on his right foot and wrap his left leg around the defensive man. Now F^2 has his back on his man and is controlling that rebounding position by forcing the defensive man toward the baseline and out of position. This puts the player in a good triangle position and he is now controlling his man after the pivot move. If we are looking at F^1 going to the baseline and having the defensive man moving toward the baseline, then F^1 would reverse pivot his left foot and wrap his right foot around his man.

Rule #3a—Baseline Adjustment Rule (Diagram 8-9)

This adjustment takes place for the most part when someone is shooting from a deep position. If the deep man decides

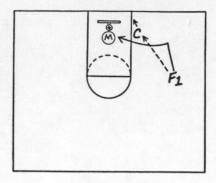

Diagram 8-9

to make his move toward the front of the basket, F^1 will apply his baseline rule. But if the deep man decides to step toward the baseline for a turn-around shot, then F^1 adjusts his path and rebounds toward the middle. This adjustment also occurs quite frequently on a fast break lay-up. We coach the baseline rebounders to adjust to the open spot in the triangle.

THE "BIG THREE" ON EVERY PLAY

The Low Post

With these few rules in mind, let us run through the low post peek play and see what develops with the rebounding. Let us see if we can put the players into the "Big Three" without making it too complicated. Remember, we want a natural flow to these positions rather than a memorized one. This will allow the players to be in the correct spots without having to break their concentration by considering too many options.

We are not going to diagram every play we have and show the "Big Three' because it would be too repetitious. Instead, we will go over certain plays and situations where we apply the different rules so that you can best understand them, and then teach these rules to your players.

The players know both the guard and deep man rules. This helps us in our zone offense and the transition game.

The Peek Play

Diagram 8-10 shows the peek play with the rebounding positions. We don't expect too many hard rebounds on a lay-up shot, so we aren't overly concerned with the garbage rebound. We do, however, have the triangle set up and the safety position covered. Notice that F^1 was going to pick his man off the center, but when he sees G^2 taking a lay-up he becomes a floating rebounder. Player F^2 follows the guard in and can either be considered a ball-side rebounder or a middle man, depending on what happens with the shot.

Diagram 8-11 illustrates the rebounding set after we run different options off the peek play. If G^1 passes the ball to F^1 as he comes around his screen, F^1 will be the ball-side rebounder and the center is the away rebounder. Player F^2 takes the middle while G^1 moves to the garbage pit and G^2 moves out to become the safety man.

If G^1 would shoot instead of passing to F^1, we would still be in the same rebounding positions with G^1 floating to the garbage areas. Player F^1 must always be aware of where the ball is and he must always hustle to his rebounding triangle position.

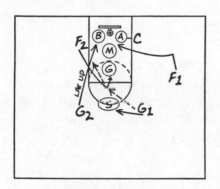

Diagram 8-10

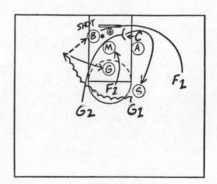

Diagram 8-11

Guard Special (Diagram 8-12)

When G^1 takes his shot after getting the ball back from the center, F^2 will take the A position on the rebound. Player F^1

will step to the middle while the center rebounds the B position. Player G^1 will float to the garbage area as G^2 takes the
safety position. Again, if G^1 and G^2 are in doubt, they both take
the garbage position and watch for the direction of the
rebound.

If F^1 decides to screen for G^2 instead of G^1, as shown in
Diagram 8-13, and G^2 takes a shot other than a lay-up, F^2 is
away, the center has ball side, and F^1 will take the middle.
Player G^2 will take the garbage while G^1 comes back out to take
the safety.

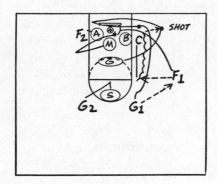
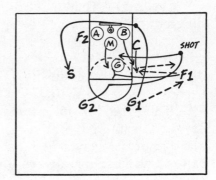

| **Diagram 8-12** | **Diagram 8-13** |

Guard Special (Center Pop)

If the center decides to pop out for the ball instead of
posting (Diagram 8-14), the rebounding assignments will
change. The big difference will be if the center will shoot rather
than pass to G^1. In this case, F^1 will rebound ball side and G^1
will step to the middle. Player G^2 will take the garbage while
the center is the safety man.

Double Screen Guard in Corner (Diagram 8-15)

After screening for G^1, the center rolls to the basket and
rebounds ball side. Player F^2 is the away rebounder and F^1 is
looking for a return pass from G^1, but doesn't get it, so he will
rebound the middle area. Player G^2 takes the safety position
while G^1 takes the garbage. Should G^1 pull up immediately
after the center's screen, then G^2 will apply the "guard rule" of

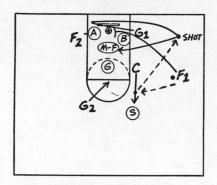 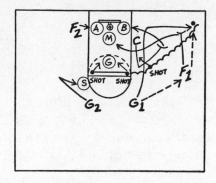

Diagram 8-14   **Diagram 8-15**

nearest to the basket and fill the garbage area. Player F^1 and G^2 are not applying the "combo rule" although F^1 is in a corner situation. Player F^1 is not shooting the ball, so he has that extra fraction of a second to get to the middle area.

Over-the-Top (Diagram 8-16)

Player G^1 passes the ball to F^1 and runs at F^1 to receive a return pass. This initial move triggers the over-the-top pass. Player F^1 will become the ball-side rebounder. The center rebounds away while F^2 applies the "deep man rule" (Rule #1) and steps to the middle. Players G^1 and G^2 at this time will apply the "guard rule."

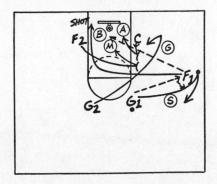

Diagram 8-16

The High Post

The rules being applied to the high post plays are exactly the same as the low post or any other set we might be in. In fact, the rules apply to all offensive situations that will occur during a ball game.

Before reading further, it might be a good idea to go back to Chapter 3 and look at the diagrams of the high post plays and see if you can apply the rules. The following checklist can be recorded on a 5 × 7 card.

1. Guard Rule (nearest to basket after shot takes the garbage).
2. Deep Man Rules (#1—step to middle; #2—float to middle).
3. Combo Rule (short corner or corner shot—guard and deep man decide who gets the middle and garbage area).
4. Baseline Rebounding (go to baseline first).
5. Baseline Adjustment Rule (go to middle).
6. Always remember rebound area first, then a man in that area.

Let's go over a few plays from the high post and see how you did with the rules.

Guard Scissor Pick (Diagram 8-17)

If F^1 passes the ball to G^2 and then G^2 drives in for the layup, F^2 has away, the center takes the middle, and F^1 floats to the garbage area, with G^1 taking the safety position.

If G^1 receives the ball after his pick off the center and shoots, F^2 is away, the center has the middle, F^1 applies the baseline rule while G^2 is clearing out to the safety position, and G^1 takes the garbage. A coach may want to make an adjustment if G^2 is a very slow guard. If he has a tough time getting to the safety position, you can then follow the guard rule of nearest guard to the basket after a shot, so G^2 takes the garbage and the other guard takes the safety.

If F^1 would pass the ball to F^2, popping around G^2's screen for a quick post shot, the center follows the rule of filling the away position first. Player F^1 uses the baseline adjustment rule, F^2 rebounds his own shot, and G^1 takes the garbage while G^2 goes to the safety position.

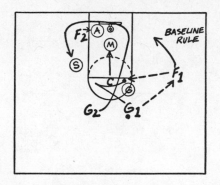

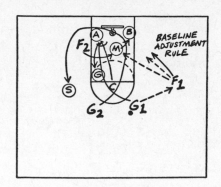

Diagram 8-17   **Diagram 8-18**

Guard-Center Double Screen Forward (Diagram 8-18)

After his screen, the center takes the away position; G^1 clears the lane and waits until the ball is shot. Then he goes to the garbage area. Player F^2 either goes all the way in for a lay-up or he takes the shot in the middle. Player G^2 will take the safety position while F^1 applies the baseline adjustment rule and rebounds either middle or ball side, depending on where F^2 takes his shot.

Guards' Double Screen Forward (Diagram 8-19)

If F^1 passes the ball to the center as he steps around G^1, then F^2 is away, the center has ball side, F^1 will use his baseline adjustment rule, and G^2 goes to the safety position while G^1 works his way to the garbage area.

Should F^1 pass the ball to F^2 coming around the twin screen, the center has away, the guards rebound the same as before, F^2 has the middle or ball side depending on where his shot is taken from, and F^1 applies the baseline adjustment rule.

Hit the Center (Diagram 8-20)

After receiving the pass from G^1, the center pivots and passes to F^2, who has wrapped his leg around his man. If F^2 shoots from the middle, the center fills the away position. If F^2 steps to the baseline for a turn-around jump shot or a power move, the center rebounds the middle. Player F^1 carries out his baseline rule, and G^2 takes the garbage as G^1 fills the safety position.

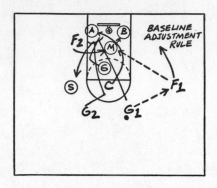 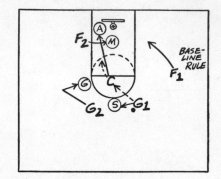

Diagram 8-19	Diagram 8-20

Rebounding in the Zone Offense (Diagram 8-21)

We will now apply the rules to the zone offense.

If 1 shoots right away, after receiving the ball from B, 2 takes the middle, 1 will float to the garbage area, and B will be the safety man.

If we are running the through pattern and 1 is taking the shot from the short corner, the rebounding position remains the same with 1 still floating to the garbage as shown in Diagram 8-21. If 2 fakes a pass to 1 as 1 arrives in the short corner, then the reverse is on, so R^1 will use R^2's screen and looks for a pass from B. After R^2 shoots the ball, 2 works his way to the away position. Player 1 will take the middle and R^1 will float to the garbage position. This is applying the combo rule (Diagram 8-22).

If 1 happens to be a forward, then we coach 1 to rebound away on the reverse and have 2 go to the middle. We would rather have the bigger men rebounding the *ball side* and *away positions*. This adjustment is made during our practice sessions. We thus know who will rebound each position on each move against zones.

If we are running the rotation and 1 takes the shot right away, R^1 and R^2 are in position already and 2 steps to the

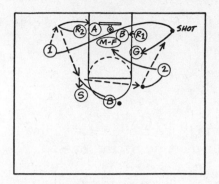

Diagram 8-21

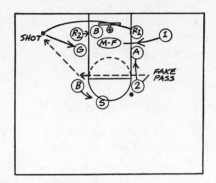

Diagram 8-22

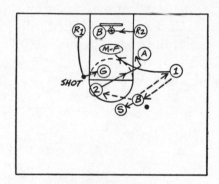

Diagram 8-23

middle to complete the triangle. Player 1 floats to the garbage and B is in the safety position, as illustrated in Diagram 8-23. If 1 passes the ball to 2 and 2 shoots the ball, R^1 and R^2 are in position, with 2 taking the middle after his shot. Player 1 floats to the garbage and B takes the safety.

If 1 has fantastic range and he shoots, then B would apply the guard rule of who is closer to the basket and he would take the garbage and 1 would be the safety.

Should 1 reverse the ball back to B as shown in Diagram 8-23, the rotation is on. If the ball is passed to R^1 as he comes up and he shoots, then 2 is away, and R^2 has ball side while 1 fills the middle my exercising his combo rule. Player R^1 will take the garbage and B has the safety position.

Most teams keep their big men near the boards when

executing their zone, so we like to keep our big men underneath. Because of this, we will make every possible adjustment to make sure we have the smaller men fill in the garbage and safety positions as much as possible.

Free Throw Rebounding

Let me share an interesting observation we've made through the years in regard to rebounding the missed free throw. We don't care if it's a grade school, high school, or college game, this observation has such a degree of accuracy that you could bet money on it. In Diagram 8-24, you see the lineup when we are shooting a free throw. Players X^1 and X^2 are the defensive players in the deep positions. Our observation is that both X^1 and X^2 will automatically go to the middle for the rebound. Not only will they move toward the middle, but they could actually touch each other. We don't know why this happens, but this holds true 95 percent of the time. We wonder if X^1 and X^2 believe that F^1 and F^2 are also going to this spot and that they must screen them out. Maybe it's because no one gives it that much thought.

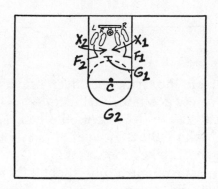

Diagram 8-24

Step Rebound

To take advantage of this, our team rebounds a little differently than most teams.

Let us concentrate on F^1's roll as a rebounder in this situation. He knows that X^1 has the advantage of the inside position to begin with, so he must do something to compensate for it (Diagram 8-24).

The first move of F^1 is to fake going to the middle and step around X^1 with his left foot. Player F^2 does the same with his right foot and G^1 has the middle to complete the triangle. The center (who shot the free throw) has the garbage and G^2 is already in the safety position.

You should see the surprised look on either X^1 or X^2's face when the rebound comes off to the side and F^1 or F^2 gets a cheap basket.

Tap Rebound (Diagram 8-25)

Now that we have shown what we are trying to do, X^1 will be making an adjustment to box out F^1, so now F^1 will fake to the outside and step inside. Player F^1 will either rebound the ball if it comes off directly to him or he will go up high and tap the ball away from X^1 with his left hand in the direction of G^1, who is moving to a short corner.

If F^2 is trying to get the inside tap from X^2, he will tap the ball with his right hand to the shooter who is moving toward the short corner as shown in Diagram 8-25. In this case, he is working with the center.

We want F^1 and F^2 to use a one-handed tap because we feel they can reach higher if they use only one arm and all they have to do is get their fingertips on the ball. This gives them a better chance against taller players.

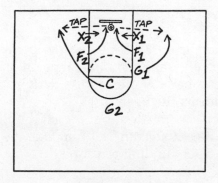

Diagram 8-25

We apply one of the two "gimmicks," as we call them, on every free throw. Our team huddles at the free throw line before every free throw. This gives them a chance to call the rebounding scheme, and we also use this time to call the different pressing techniques we use after a missed or made free throw. We have used calls like 21, where the first digit means the left side and the second means the right side. So on a 21 call, F^2 and the shooter work together to tap the ball out, and F^1 works alone stepping around X^1.

If we call 12, then F^2 steps around and F^1 and G^1 work together on the tap. The signal 11 would have both F^1 and F^2 stepping around X^1 and X^2, with G^1 going to the middle while the shooter takes garbage.

We hope there won't be too many missed free throws by our team in a game. Therefore, we are talking about taking advantage of the opportunity to rebound the few missed ones. The normal effectiveness of rebounding by the team shooting a free throw is 30 percent, according to our stats. This low percentage is caused mostly by the fact that the opponents fill the deep inside position so they have the advantage, and most free throws don't come bounding off hard like some other shots might.

Since we instilled these gimmicks, we raised our effectiveness to 45 percent. Again, this fits into our rebounding philosophy of taking every opportunity to gain the advantage when rebounding.

SUMMARY

If we are playing against a zone and the perimeter shooting is off, we use our rebounding as an extension of the offense. We have been described by the sports writers as a team that "shoots and storms the boards."

If we are off on our shooting, we get the ball to the shooter who has the softest touch and let him take the shots. Then we go to our tough rebounding to score.

A coach once told us that his team had trouble with certain zones because his guards were poor perimeter shooters and they couldn't get the ball inside because they were poor passers. His best outside shooter was the toughest rebounder and he didn't want to bring him outside.

We told him to "shoot and storm the boards." Let the deep men rebound tough and score from inside. If you think about it, even the poorest outside shooter will make some of his shots—add that to your rebounding points and you are back in the ball game.

One year we had a guard who shot under 40 percent, but who had a nice, soft shot. He was willing to take the shots and our other men rebounded tough. As a result, the guard made all-state and we went to the state tournament with a 21-3 record, with every loss coming in overtime. That was truly a year of shooting and storming the boards.

The multiple rules might seem too numerous and complicated to remember, but these rules are actually very much common sense to the players. Therefore, the players catch on quickly after a few repetitions and "insistence" reminders. Furthermore, the players like the benefit of knowing exactly where they should be on a given shot and also can check themselves when they are not in the proper position.

We don't have the players memorize their rebounding positions on every play. Instead we teach them the fundamental rules and principles to follow, and this takes them into a natural feel for where to be when a shot is taken.

The rebounding positions are built right into the system, when we free lance or fast break the rules come in handy. We can make adjustments during a game because we have something to fall back on. We don't believe in letting players choose their own rebounding positions. We always want the best percentage rebounding positions, namely "The Big Three."

As a coach, you should emphasize in practice the necessity of getting a triangle on each shot. Your stressing of the rules will allow the players to catch on quickly through repetition and the natural logic of the positions.

9

USING THE PICK-AND-SCREEN
IN SPECIAL SITUATIONS

We interpret anything that takes us away from the normal Pick-and-Screen attack as a special situation. In this chapter we will discuss how we attack these situations using the Pick-and-Screen as needed.

PICK APART THE FULL-COURT
MAN-TO-MAN PRESS

It was mentioned in Chapter 6 that any pressure higher than midcourt is treated as full-court pressure, which means that the entire team moves up to run some unique plays. We also realize that a good dribbling guard can just dribble one-on-one down the court while his teammates clear the area. At this point we just want to show some moves that the entire team can get involved in when a team doesn't have those super one-on-one players. The plays can also be used by a team that likes to strike quickly.

The 21 Set—Pick Off the Guard

Diagram 9-1 shows the lineup and the initial picks using the 21 set. We have numbered this set 21 because we have two players picking off the one player.

When G^2 slaps the ball, the player on the side of the ball (F^2) breaks first, and F^1 is the second cutter. Player G^1 is facing the center when the ball is out of bounds. By facing upcourt, he knows when the cutters have gone by him, so he can now go put a belly-up screen on the man guarding the center. The center picks his man off the screen and moves up toward the top of the key. Player G^2 has the option of passing the ball to F^1, F^2, or the center, depending on who is open. No matter whom G^2 passes to, he will cut right by that player to either receive a return pass or to fill the lane for the player he passes to.

What we would like to do is get the ball in the middle of the court as soon as possible. Diagram 9-2 shows G^2 passing

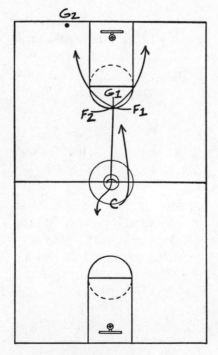

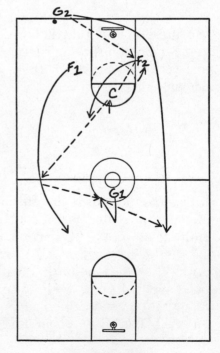

Diagram 9-1   **Diagram 9-2**

the ball to F^2 and cutting right by him. Player F^2 pivots after receiving the pass and looks for the center in the middle of the court. Player F^2 passes the ball to the center and cuts right by him. After receiving the pass, the center pivots and looks for F^1 moving down the back-side lane. After G^1 screens for the center, G^1 works his way down court and he then times his move back toward the ball so F^1 can find him for a pass to the middle. If G^1 receives a pass from F^1, G^1 looks for G^2 filling the back-side lane. You will notice in Diagram 9-2 that F^2 is breaking by the center after his pass, looking for a return pass or filling the middle lane.

Diagrams 9-3 and 9-4 illustrate the movement of the ball should G^2 pass to the center or F^1. No matter which player receives the pass, the center or F^1 look for someone to pass to. If no one is open, they are allowed to dribble the ball with their heads up looking for a teammate breaking to the middle. We want the man filling the lane away from the ball to be ready to

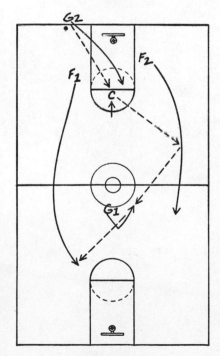

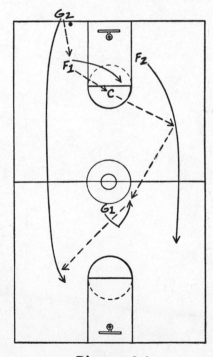

Diagram 9-3   **Diagram 9-4**

come back to the middle area. Diagram 9-5 shows a situation where the center looked for an open man but was forced to dribble. Player F^2 was away from the ball so he breaks to the middle and toward the center to receive a pass from the center. If F^2 receives the pass, he looks for F^1 filling the back side lane.

When lining up in the 21 set, the forwards are coached to free themselves any way they can. If the defense is anticipating that they are going to complete a full scissor, they can start the scissor, but then break directly to the ball. Over a period of time practicing this set, the forwards get to know what they can do to free themselves for the initial inbounds pass.

Once we clear the half-court line, we will take advantage of any situation that will lead us directly to a basket. If we can't score immediately, we set up our Pick-and-Screen offense.

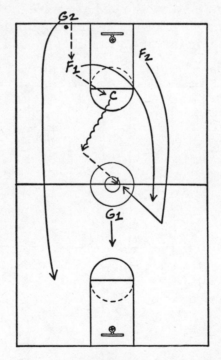

Diagram 9-5

22 Box Set

Diagram 9-6 illustrates the lineup and the initial moves when we are running the 22 set. When G^2 slaps the ball, F^1 and

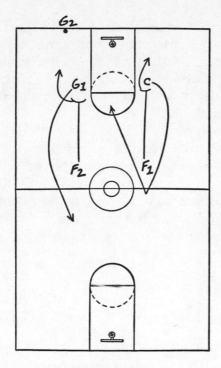

Diagram 9-6

F^2 move up to put on a belly-up screen. Player G^1 and the center wait for the screeners to get all the way up to them before they release down court. Player G^2 looks for G^1 to see if he is open for a long pass. If G^1 is open, G^2 will throw the ball to the opposite free throw line rather than trying to hit G^1 on the move. Player G^1 will run to that spot expecting the ball to be there. We find it easier to complete this play if G^2 has a stationary target (i.e., the far free throw line) to pass to rather than a moving one.

Diagram 9-6 shows our secondary moves if we can't throw the bomb. Players F^1 and F^2, after screening, will move toward the sideline to open up the middle lane. Player G^1, the man on the side of the ball, will break all the way to the basket. The man away from the ball, in this case our center, only breaks to the midcourt. Then the center breaks back toward the ball looking for a pass from G^2. Player G^2 has the option of passing to anyone that is open. Once G^2 makes his initial pass, all the options for moving the ball down court are the same as in the 21 set.

If the defense is playing in front of F^1 or F^2 (between G^2 with the ball and F^1 or F^2 at the start of the play), F^1 or F^2 have the option of raising their hand (closed fist) to signal to G^2 that they are open, and G^2 has the option of passing the ball to the far free throw line while the player that signals runs to that area to receive the long pass.

We want each player to be able to play any of the positions in this set. That way we can rotate players around so the defense cannot zero in on any one player or any particular move we want to make. We interchange the 21 and 22 series by running one play several times and then suddenly switching to the other set. We thus often catch the opponent unaware in this switch and find that we get some easy baskets.

THE TANDEM ATTACK AGAINST FULL-COURT ZONE DEFENSES

In Chapter 6 we explained how we used the tandem against midcourt zones. This same set is just as effective against full-court zone presses. Diagram 9-7 shows the tandem set against 2-2-1 full-court zone. The two tandem players are coached to stay in the heart (middle) of the zone. They make their adjustments according to how high or low the zone sits. Player G^2 will pass to G^1 and F^1 is coached to break to the ball side. Player F^1 breaks toward the sideline behind the front defensive man. At this time, F^2 steps up in the middle as shown in Diagram 9-7. If G^1 cannot pass to F^2, he will pass back to G^2 and F^2 will break toward the sideline while F^1 breaks back to the middle. If the ball is passed to F^1, F^1 looks for G^1 breaking down the back side lane. The only thing that would change the initial moves would be if the defense would pressure G^1 on the inbound pass and he could not receive the ball. Player G^2 would still be holding the ball so he becomes ball side, and F^1 will break to that side and F^2 will step up into the middle area.

We insist that the players get the ball to the middle as soon as possible. We feel that from the middle of the court there are better and more passing lanes and the chances of being trapped are minimized.

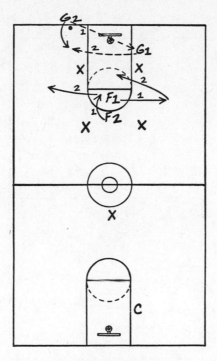

Diagram 9-7

The use of insistent coaching over a period of time results in the ball moving down court very quickly and smoothly. Once the ball is deep in the front court, we either go directly to the basket or we set up the Pick-and-Screen offense.

THE 23 SET ATTACKS
THE FULL-COURT ZONE DEFENSES

Diagram 9-8 depicts the lineup in the 23 set. If there is an opening in the middle of the zone, the center steps up and G^2 passes him the ball. The center looks for F^1 going back side. With F^2 going down the other side, we have a two-on-one break. If there isn't an opening in the middle, G^2 passes to G^1. He is coached not to be in a hurry to get down the court because we believe that there will be another man open if we just take our time.

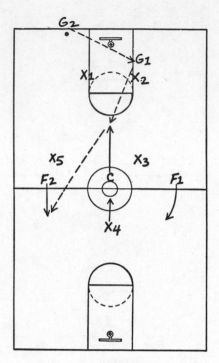

Diagram 9-8

We don't want anyone dribbling down the sideline. By dribbling down the sideline we feel that we give the defense an easy trap or pin. So, G^1 is instructed to keep the ball as close to the middle of the court as possible. When G^1 is handling the ball, he will study the defense looking for F^1, F^2, or the center to pass the ball to. If they are not open, G^1 passes back to G^2, who looks for the same options.

It will take no more than two passes until one of the three are open. No matter how the defense plays, after the first pass to the player at midcourt, there is always a two-on-one break. If we can't score on the break, we go right into the Pick-and-Screen offense.

A good coaching point using the 23 set is if X^5 on the defense moves up close to the midcourt and if one of the defensive men is playing in front of F^1 or F^2, then F^1 or F^2 has the option of raising his hand in a closed fist. In Diagram 9-8 the defensive man in F^2's area has moved in front of him to take the direct pass away, so F² raises a closed fist. Player G² now has the option of throwing the bomb to the opposite free throw lane.

THE QUICK FAST BREAK

Teams that scout us know that 99 percent of the time, when they pressure us, we are going to take enough time getting the ball out of bounds so that we can set up the full-court offense. They are also convinced that they have enough time to set up their defense to stop our offensive attack. What they don't know is when we are going to run our quick fast break. The guards normally take the ball out of bounds. On the quick fast break the man nearest the basket takes the ball as it comes through the net and jumps out of bounds outside of the free throw lane. He looks for the guards releasing down court. While the defense is looking for us to set up, we are scoring at the other end.

If the player taking the ball out of bounds cannot throw the bomb, he looks for the other two big men who are in the immediate area of the back court, depending on where they end up on their defensive play. If a big man gets the ball, he looks deep first, or then looks for one of the guards coming back toward the ball. The guard coming back is the guard whose defensive man has beaten him down the court. If this happens, the guard works his way back to midcourt. We want the ball to get across the midcourt line as quickly as possible.

After we do this a couple of times, we go back to taking our time while setting up the full-court offense.

The quick fast break drill will be shown in Chapter 11.

This change of pace move goes well with the set-up attack. We like to use the quick break when we think the defense is starting to anticipate our set move. It works well against man-to-man presses and it is even more effective against a team that zone presses. By not letting the defense set up, a team can score some easy baskets. The quick break is usually set up during a time-out, when we can get everyone's attention as to what we are going to do.

THE PICK IN TRANSITION—FAST BREAK

All we ask of the players in the fast break is to fill the lanes and get the ball in the middle as soon as possible. We want all the lanes to be filled by the time the break gets to midcourt. This is accomplished by constant drilling on rebounding, the outlet pass, and the filling of all the lanes as we move the ball down court. The fast break drills are illustrated in Chapter 11.

3-on-2 Break

By the time we reach the midcourt line, we have all three lanes filled, plus a trailer following the ball in the middle lane. At all times we have a safety man whose job is to make sure that every one of the opponents are ahead of him on the break. Diagram 9-9 depicts the alignment as we approach the free throw area. Insistent coaching has taken over at this point. All the lanes are filled, the ball is in the middle, the trailer is in position, and the safety man is back.

The first option for the player with the ball is to penetrate to the basket. If he can't drive all the way but penetrates past the free throw line, he is coached to shoot right *now*! As it is illustrated in Chapter 10, we believe that once you cross the free throw line you are in the highest possible percentage position on the floor. So we naturally want the player to penetrate past the free throw line and shoot the ball. If he cannot penetrate, he looks for G^1 and F^2 crossing underneath the basket. We want the man on the right side to cut just in front of the basket and the man on the left to go through the basket. Player G^1 is actually using a running screen so that F^2 can pick his defensive man off, as is shown in Diagram 9-9. If G^2 can't penetrate, he has the option of moving to the right side of the lane looking first for F^2, then G^1, and finally for the trailer, who fills in on the left of the lane (Diagram 9-9).

Fast Breaking Against the Two-Man Tandem Defense

When trying to stop the three-on-two break, most teams will have their two men challenge the break by lining up in a tandem set (Diagram 9-10).

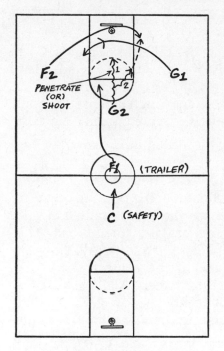

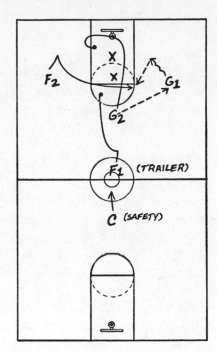

Diagram 9-9   **Diagram 9-10**

As soon as G^2 reads that the defense is in a tandem, he passes the ball to G^1 or F^2. Player G^2 then slides to the basket on the ball side looking for a return pass. If G^2 does not receive a pass he moves to a spot on the other side of the basket. If G^1 has the ball, he makes sure that the defense comes out to stop his penetration before he looks to pass to F^2. Player F^2 starts for the basket, then cuts across the lane to the end of the free throw line looking for a pass from G^1. If F^2 gets the ball, he looks first to shoot, and then for G^2 on the other side of the basket.

The trailer fills in at the other end of the free throw line and acts as a safety valve when no one else is open for the shot. When using this move, we find that F^2 usually ends up with a good percentage shot. The next best option is getting the ball to G^2 as he moves away from the ball. If the defense recovers and catches up with the fast break, then the trailer is the one who usually ends up with the shot.

OUT-OF-BOUNDS PLAYS

We try to score every time we take the ball out of bounds. Over the years we have scored directly from the out-of-bounds plays six out of every ten times we have taken the ball out. The four times we fail is due to missed shots or a tough defense. It seems that the simpler we keep the plays, the more effective they are.

Beneath the Basket (Diagram 9-11)

We use this 22 set against zones as well as against man-to-man defenses. We put the best shooter in the position occupied by F^1 in the diagram. When F^2 slaps the ball, F^1 moves toward him, extending his arms out and begging for the ball. This forces the defender to move between F^1 and the ball. Now the defender is set up to be picked off the center. The center doesn't have to put on any particular screen. All he has to do is take up room so that the defender cannot get by. We want F^1 to break out only to the short corner if possible when he comes around the center's screen. After F^2 passes the ball to F^1, F^2 will become the away rebounder. If F^1 cannot get the shot, he looks for the center posting.

When F^1 starts the play by begging for the ball, F^2 can pass him the ball if he is open on this initial move. Player F^1 can also give some kind of hand signal to F^2 and then step like he's going to go by the center and then break back to the basket for a pass from F^2.

We also use this set against any type of zones. When working against a zone, the center is coached to stay outside of the widest defender on the zone. On the slap of the ball, the center puts a belly-up screen on the widest man and F^1 comes around the center for a short corner shot. After the center screens, he pivots around facing F^1 looking for a pass if F^1 cannot shoot. Again, F^2 becomes the away rebounder.

Most teams that use this type of set usually have F^1 screening for the center, while the center breaks to the open side. When F^1 looks like he is going to screen for the center but continues on by him, F^1 is usually open for the shot.

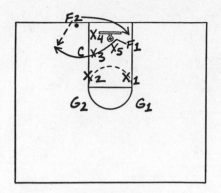

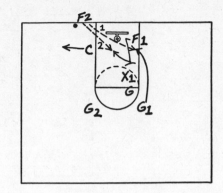

Diagram 9-11   Diagram 9-12

For a change of pace, F^1 will screen for G^1 and then F^1 will roll to the basket (Diagram 9-12). When the center sees F^1 going up to screen, he widens out so there is more room under the basket. If G^1 is not open, then F^2 looks for F^1 rolling to the basket. These are the only two plays we use underneath the basket, but they are very successful. The first option of F^1 breaking by the center is the most productive option.

Sideline (Out of Bounds) (Diagram 9-13)

Player F^2 passes the ball to G^2 and uses the belly-up screen set by F^1 to pick his man off. Player F^1 then heads for the basket. Player G^2 passes the ball to G^1 and G^1 looks for F^2. We want F^2 to receive the pass just as he clears the basket. Player F^2 will also take a short step with his right foot toward the free throw line. Player F^2 here uses the same technique as he does in the low post peek series. He is coached to wrap his leg around so that he keeps the defensive man on his back. Most players will have a tendency to go outside of the free throw area to receive the pass. A coach must insist that their players wrap their legs if the play is to be successful. If F^2 is not open, G^1 will look for F^1 coming over the top of the center. If F^2 cannot inbound the ball to G^2, F^2 can pass to the center and the center can pass to G^1. We want G^1 to handle the ball so that the man guarding him cannot sag and cut off the passing lane to

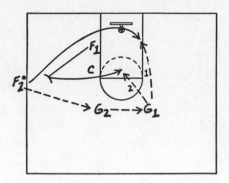

Diagram 9-13

F^2. This is a simple play but very effective. If the initial pass to G^2 seems impossible, G^2 can screen for G^1 and G^1 then breaks toward F^2 for the pass. If G^1 receives the ball he looks to pass to G^2. Player G^2, after receiving the ball, looks for F^2 underneath or F^1 coming over the top of the center.

SUMMARY

The diagrams in this chapter tend to lead to the conclusion that a coach must place his players in the exact positions that they appear in the diagrams or his team will not obtain the best results. The diagrams were designed in such a way so everything is in a balanced order. In our system, we place our players in positions where they can perform to their maximum. For instance, if we are going to throw the bomb, we want a player taking the ball out who can throw the bomb.

We call our set the 22 set. The opponents call it the "Box." When we go into this set and hear the opponent's bench hollering "Watch out for the Box, watch out for the Box," we know that we have something good going for us. If the opponents stay in a full-court man-to-man press the full game, our players know they are going to average their normal three baskets during a game on the bomb alone.

We get away with the long pass because we interchange the positions of the players so often that these changes invaria-bly result in someone falling asleep on defense.

If the defense is playing a full-court zone defense, we will use the tandem attack about one-third of the time and the 23 set the other two-thirds of the time. We like the 23 set because as the ball is being passed between the guards, one of the three players at half-court is always open. This results in the two-on-one breaks that any team wants to have.

Opponents pick us up full court to try and counter the Pick-and-Screen offense. Because of this we have developed the counterattack of our own that is discussed and diagrammed in this chapter. As a result, we have neutralized the full-court presses and, in most cases, caused the defense to try some other method to beat us.

10

BUILDING THE PICK-AND-SCREEN OFFENSE

While building this system we have instilled our own philosophy of coaching in the Pick-and-Screen offense. Although our own coaching personalities are embedded in this system, its success can be a result of a combination of a coach's own beliefs and his personal commitment to the fundamental disciplines of shooting, dribbling, passing, and rebounding.

Most coaches seem to agree that it is not the system but the execution of the system that makes the difference. We like to believe that it is a combination of both. We believe that a good player competing in a poor system will not necessarily play to his capabilities. On the other hand, a poor player playing in a sound system can be competitive.

To us, a good system is something that a coach's personality can be identified with. It is something that the players thoroughly believe in. It is something that can be used year after year with only minor adjustments in a particular series to take advantage of the special abilities of each player.

The Pick-and-Screen is this type of system. It is a disciplined offense that has so many options that it is adaptable to any style of play.

We would like to think we alone developed this offense as it is illustrated in this book. But we know from experience that (without really knowing it) we were highly influenced by some fine coaches in the early development of this offense. Since that time we have modified their thoughts into our own system.

Although everything we talk about in this chapter is geared to our way of thinking, a coach can put his own thoughts and personality into this system and make it work. However, the things we will discuss are backed up by years of gathering statistics and observing the little things that make a good offense. We also believe that parts of a good offense are the results of a coach's own defensive philosophy. For instance, if you know that your defense has a tough time stopping a certain move, you will very likely have that move in your offense. On the other hand, if you stop a certain play consistently, you will discard that play from your offense.

INSTALLING THE DISCIPLINE NEEDED FOR THE PICK-AND-SCREEN OFFENSE

Because shooting is so important to any offense, we spend a lot of time with our players on *How*, *What*, *Where*, and *When* to shoot.

Shooting

The How of Shooting

The following are the guidelines for the shooters:

1. Square up feet and hips to the basket; bend knees.
2. Spread fingers comfortably on the ball; place only the finger-tips on the ball.
3. Keep shooting hand under and in back of the ball, while using off hand to protect and steady the ball.
4. Form a "C" with upper arm, forearm, and hand when looking at the side view of the shooter.

5. Line up hand, forearm, and elbow as closely as possible to the mid-line of the body. Do not move elbow out to the side.

6. Center head on a mid-point line between the feet.

7. Keep eyes on the basket.

8. Roll the ball off the fingertips on the shot. Back spin results in a soft shot.

9. Shoot out of the "phone booth." The shot should be up and out rather than out and up. This helps with the trajectory or arc of the shot.

10. Snap the wrist; reach into the basket.

11. Keep the arm extended after the shot for a proper follow-through.

What to Shoot

The following shots are the only shots we allow our players to practice or use in a game.

1. Jump Shot: The shooter follows all the guidelines for shooting while jumping as high as possible on every shot. The shooter should come down on the same spot he jumped from. He should maintain the same arm stroke no matter where he shoots from. When the shot becomes an arm shot instead of a leg shot, the shooter is out of his range.

2. Set Shot: Some players still use it for their long-range shot. Use the same technique as a jump shot without leaving the floor.

3. Lay-up: Keep two hands on the ball as long as possible before releasing the ball. Go straight up and be able to catch the ball coming through the net. This helps you to get maximum height. It also means that you won't overrun the basket and take yourself out of a rebounding position. Place the ball high and soft on the board.

4. Cross Over: Lay the ball up while crossing to the opposite side of the basket while turning the hips into the basket. Be able to catch the ball coming through the net.

5. Swing Shot: This is a hook shot without stepping away from the basket. This shot is used when a player is going toward the basket and a defensive man is in the lane. The

shooter swings the ball over the top of the defender. It is also used if a player is going across the lane (close to the basket) and swings over a taller player.

6. Hook Shot: We don't encourage our players to shoot this shot, but they are permitted to practice this type of shot (at short range) if they are capable of shooting it.

7. Power Dribble-Power Shot: This shot is used while posting or taking a rebound off the board and moving closer to the basket. When posting, the shooter drop-steps to the basket, driving the ball to the floor with both hands and keeping the ball next to his lead foot while in a low position. The shooter is now ready to power jump into his shot. The post man can also step toward the front of the basket while using the same technique. We coach the shooter to take the power shot right to his man rather than using a fade-away shot. We insist that all our players work on and use this type of shot.

The types of shots that we *never* accept are an underhand lay-up, a fade-away, or any other shot that does not fall under our defined techniques.

This statement might shock some coaches, but according to our statistical data, the underhand lay-up, fade-away, and others are shots that range from an average of 25 percent to 35 percent accuracy, so we consider them poor percentage shots. We insist that our players do not take them.

Where to Shoot

We assign a percentage figure on each type of shot our players take and a percentage mark for shooting areas on the floor. Our statistics have always backed us up. Our findings over a period of years and our experience with these statistics show that the percentages haven't fluctuated more than a couple of points in either direction.

Coaches and players are shocked by these set percentages and naturally at first do not believe that they are true. It doesn't take long for our own players to become believers as the practices begin and after playing a few games.

Diagram 10-1 depicts the positions on the floor that are high percentage areas. The actual positions vary a step or two one way or the other. We consider anything under 45 percent a

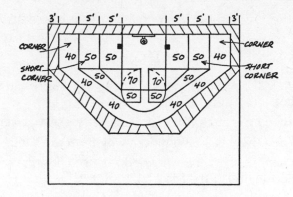

Diagram 10-1

low percentage shot and will discourage that shot from being taken. The shaded area near the baseline is known as the backboard line and no shots are allowed in that area.

The areas shaded three feet from the sidelines and twenty-two feet or more from the basket are also areas in which we discourage the players from taking shots.

The area down the middle and to the immediate left and right of the basket are left up to an individual coach's discretion. They can be considered lay-up lanes or power shooting positions.

A player's individual talents to score with his back to the basket will also dictate his assigned percentage in these positions. We insist that our players do not take a lay-up directly over the front rim. That shot falls under the 40 percent limit.

When to Shoot

We let our players know which shots are high percentage shots for them, and we never discourage their shooting from the high percentage areas on the floor. An example would be in a fast break situation where any player has the ball at the 70 percent or 50 percent positions shown in Diagram 10-1. We encourage him to shoot at those positions. We will, however, discourage a player from taking a shot out of his range and encourage a good shooter to take a shot in a lesser percentage area if he has the range. Some of the "when" to shoot is left up to a coach's own philosophy about: (1) time on the clock; (2)

score of the game; and (3) a coach's own game strategies for winning.

When do we allow our players to shoot?:

1. When the player is in his range and he has confidence in that shot.
2. When he is in a position to take his highest percentage shot.
3. When there is a rebounder away from the shot.
4. When the shooter is in a good balanced position and is able to execute one of the acceptable shots.

Passing

You will hear the comment, "He is surely a good passer," more often than, "They are a good passing team." Not everyone on a team is a great passer. But everyone on the team will be handling the ball at some time during the game. With this in mind, we set up some guidelines for the players to follow so that they can all become at least adequate passers.

Passing Rules

The six rules we always insist on are:

1. Always look to the basket before passing. There might be someone open underneath. This will also force the defense to sag off so the passing lanes on the perimeter will open up. Keep the ball at chin level so that you are a triple threat.
2. Do not look one way and pass the other way. Some players believe if they completely turn their heads away, they will fool the defense.
3. Do not pass the ball so that the man catching it is taken out of his fundamental shooting position or shooting range.
4. When fast breaking or while stealing a ball, never pass to a man heading for the baseline in the shot corner or corner as shown in Diagram 10-2. This pass will cause the man receiving the ball to run himself past the backboard line into the no shooting area.
5. In some situations a good fake pass is as good as a pass. It can create passing lanes to the inside or the perimeter.

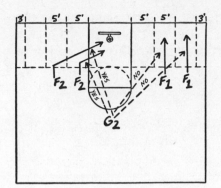

Diagram 10-2

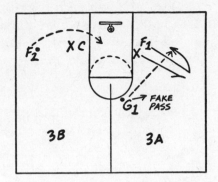

Diagram 10-3b   Diagram 10-3a

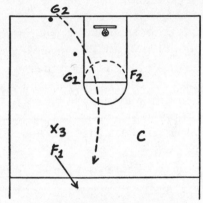

Diagram 10-3c

6. At all times watch for the closed-fist signal given by the man you are trying to pass to. It means that he wants to break to the basket.

a. Diagram 10-3a shows F^1 breaking to the wing position. He is being denied the pass by the defensive player X^1. Player F^1 shows a closed fist with his target hand (left hand) and breaks for the basket. Player G^1 sees the closed fist, so he fakes the pass to F^1 and looks for him breaking to the basket.

b. Diagram 10-3b depicts the center being fronted while he is posting. The center makes a closed fist with his target hand and that is the signal that he wants the ball over the top.

c. Diagram 10-3c illustrates the defensive man X^3 playing in front of F^1 on the 22 full-court man-to-man set. Against a full-court press F^1 raises his hand and closes his fist. This signal gives G^2 the option of passing the ball to the free throw circle on the other end of the court.

By signalling with the closed fist, we have eliminated the "I thought" excuse that players use so often. It has really helped in cutting down on our turnovers and in the scoring of some easy baskets.

Dribbling

We want dribbling to be an extension of our passing. The basic rules are:

1. Use the dribble to get out of trouble, not into trouble.
2. Never dribble into the corner.
3. Don't dribble close to the sideline. Keep the ball in the middle one-third of the court as much as possible. This way you have more directions in which you can dribble, and the defense cannot pin you to the sideline.
4. If you catch a pass in any place on the court (not in a posting position) with your back to the basket, don't dribble the ball until after you turn and face the basket. This will keep you from being trapped, and you will not dribble off someone's foot. It also follows the rule of looking to the basket when you receive a pass.
5. Use the dribble to create better passing angles.

Rebounding

To be a good rebounder, you must want to rebound all the time. This is what we stress to the players. We don't want any chance rebounds. You have to work harder for an offensive rebound position because of the advantage the defensive men have by being in the inside position to start with. In our offense we rebound an area first, and then a man in that area. Chapter 8 explained the rules and areas to be rebounded.

Guidelines for Rebounding

1. Rebound with two hands. Besides having better control of the rebound, you will have more power.
2. Never stand behind or alongside (hip to hip) anyone while rebounding. Always work for a position where the middle line of your back is touching the man in your area. You might

never get inside the man in your area but you can *always* get halfway around him.

3. Bend knees slightly, keep back straight, and hands up to at least shoulder height.

4. Study the flight of the ball to determine where the missed shot will come off. That way you can keep your back on your man.

5. Time your jump so you rebound the ball at your highest possible vertical jump.

6. When coming down with the ball, maintain your position (back on your man). Be ready to bounce quickly off your toes and go right back up for a shot or use a power dribble to get closer to the basket. If neither opportunity is there, pass the ball to a perimeter man. If you cannot control the ball, keep it alive by tipping it to the basket or a teammate.

7. If the ball is coming down farther away from the basket than your position, move under the ball before you go up. Don't reach for it with one hand.

Posting

The posting area is a position on the big block of the free throw lane. We believe that if someone posts higher than that, the defensive man can get his arm and body around the man posting, thereby cutting off the passing lane. If he positions himself lower than the block, the defensive man can stay on the high side, again cutting off the passing lane and pinning your post man to the baseline.

At a position on the block, the post man has plenty of room to take the drop-step to the basket or a step to the middle of the lane using a power dribble and a power shot. He is also close enough to the basket to shoot a turn-around jump shot.

In this offense, if a player posts anywhere but on the block, that player is not trying to score but is setting up another player for a shot.

We do a lot of posting in the Pick-and-Screen, but it is not the primary attack, so we coach the players not to force the ball into the post. We are not going to lose a game because we can't get the ball into the post. The post is there to help the perimeter game and the perimeter game in return helps the post play.

Between the posting and the flashing through the lane after the screen, you have enough of an inside game to go along with the perimeter play.

There are different schools of thought on how a player should post up. Some say that he should be in a low position and others say he should be in a straight-up position. We use both positions, depending on whether the defense is playing on the high side, the low side, or fronting the post man. We want the man posting to have his knees and back slightly bent with his target hand waist high. His upper arm should be at a 45 degree angle from his body and his forearm parallel to the floor. In this position it is harder for the defensive man to reach around the post man and deflect the ball. We want the ball to come in at the knee away from the defensive man.

Players have a tendency to believe that the only way to feed a post man is to pass the ball over the top of the man guarding the passer. As a result, they hold the ball over their head and lob the pass.

With the ball over head, the passer takes away his first option, which is to shoot. The defensive man can either crowd him or sag and help with the post, knowing that the man with the ball cannot dribble or shoot with the ball that high in the air.

We coach the players feeding the post to keep the ball in a threat position, namely, at chin level. The ball can get to the post by a direct pass from the man with the ball or by the feeder's using a dribble to create a better passing lane. The man with the ball can also pass the ball to someone on the perimeter who has a better passing angle to the post.

If the defense is fronting the post man, then we want him in a straight-up, one-half turn position with his target hand up over his head. When the man posting wants the ball, he will show a closed fist. The man with the ball now has the option of passing him the ball if he sees that the defense will give no back-side help.

We don't want the post man moving once he sets himself on the block. If the post man is moving up and down the line to get a better position, so is the defensive man. Now the passer has to read two people. The feeder is responsible for getting the ball to the post. He does this by using the pass or the dribble to create passing angles.

Building the Offense—Day One

The preceding check points for the players are the foundation of the offense.

We are very fortunate to have a freshman team in our school. The day we officially can start practice we have a two-day basketball camp for the freshman team. Our entire staff is used to teach the basic guidelines and fundamentals. At this time we instill in the players our way of thinking and what we expect from each one of them if they want to be part of the Pick-and-Screen system.

After the freshman camp, we have a two-day camp for the sophomores, juniors, and seniors. During this time we won't run through any patterns, but we instill the discipline needed to run this offense.

In the first practice as a team we run through the entire offense. It is our belief that after a player understands the whole concept, he will better understand the need for breaking the offense down to single plays. Finally, he will realize the need to set up drills to improve his own individual fundamental skills, which are needed to execute the offense.

Now we start using the drills (Chapter 11) as part of our practice time. Each drill is designed to help the offense. We introduce the fast break drills and the full-court pressure offense as soon as possible. Besides using these drills to learn the proper techniques, they are used for conditioning. We don't believe in wasting practice time getting players in condition by using drills that have no bearing on the offense. We insist that the players get into condition on their own time. We might stay after practice three or four times a season to test their stamina.

When working on the offense we always work five men at a time. All five men are responsible for its success or failure, so they always work together. In a particular situation only two or three players are screening or picking; however, the remaining players are ready for the second and third options and are setting up for their rebounding responsibilities.

We have never been able to come up with a drill that could be useful to the players away from the ball except five-on-five play. We will, however, take one play at a time and run it over and over until we are satisfied with the results. When you can consistently run a play with success while the defense is doing everything possible to stop it, you know that play has some value in your offense.

We do break down for the drills that are designed to help each player with his basic fundamentals. These fundamentals together with good play selection form a sound offense.

If we are going to play against a good trapping defense or against a team that is much faster than we are, we will run the offense against six or seven defenders. It makes the offense hustle more and forces them to concentrate on the different options.

Developing the Little Man (Quarterback)

Extra time has to be spent with the guards because they are considered second coaches out on the court. They must understand the Pick-and-Screen system and know the strengths and weaknesses of each player, including themselves. It would not be smart basketball if a guard would set himself up for a double screen in the corner knowing his range is limited. He must also know his strengths and limitations on his dribbling and passing. Once he knows these limitations and strengths, he is ready to take over the offense. This doesn't mean he won't be trying to improve on his weaknesses during the season. It does mean, however, that he must not put himself or his teammates in a situation that works against the execution of the offense. Once the player's skills are evaluated at the beginning of the season, we select the plays out of our playbook that are best suitable to them at that time.

We then sit down with the guards and go over the plays selected and all the situations that can occur. This could be compared to a football coach developing his quarterback. In the early season, we do this on a regular basis. As we approach the first game, we go over special situations in regard to time-outs, last-second shots, and so on. With all this information, a dedication to the drills, and the ever-present insistent coaching, the guards are ready to run the Pick-and-Screen offense.

The Use of Stat Sheets to Build the Program

A lot of coaches say that "statistics are for losers." We like to believe that a coach can use them to build a winning team.

We realize a coach who has a good program doesn't need statistics to tell him that the team is functioning at a high or low level. We also know that not all players can evaluate their own performances. Therefore, we use statistics more for the players than for the coaches. We also use statistics to build a mental toughness that will help improve an individual player's performance.

We go from individual, to team, to school career statistics to motivate the players. When we started these statistics 19 years ago, we didn't want to get so involved that we would need an expert analyst to interpret them, so we limited the offensive statistics to the following:

Individual

1. Field goal percentage
   a. Points per game
2. Free throw percentage
3. Offensive rebound average
4. The last-pass average

Team

1. Field goal percentage
2. Points per game
3. Offensive rebound average

Every two years we also publish a pamphlet of statistics with team and individual records in every category we can think of. They are sent to each alumnus who has his name in it. Besides being good public relations with the alumni, the sports writers like to know about someone breaking a school record.

What these stats mean to us is that we have to help each player pick his shooting spots and that each player must work hard to get the majority of his shots in those areas. In practice he must work on those shots in order to improve on his field goal percentage.

What has helped us with our shooting is the fact that we never allow the players to shoot alone. They are always working with someone, either in competition with each other or against another group of players. We found that competitive shooting helped the percentage shooting more than the lazy shooting habits acquired by players when they were allowed to shoot on their own. To make sure that they are accomplishing this, we go as a team to the gym to start practice and when practice is over we leave the gym together. We also carry this competition over to the free throw shooting. We always shoot one-and-one when shooting free throws. The players will always challenge each other. A typical challenge would be ten finger tip push-ups if the first free throw is missed and five if the second is missed. We set aside two different times in practice to shoot free throws. We want the players shooting them early in practice to represent the first half of a game and then late in practice when they are tired to simulate the last few minutes in a game.

You have noticed that we put the individual's point average in its proper place, i.e., a subdivision of field goal percentages. We know that one player is going to score more than another. What we don't want is what we call a "gunner" on the team. That is a player who takes a lot of shots during a game trying to build up his point average while his shooting percentage is way below par.

We set scoring and percentage goals for each of the players. We make them realistic enough that they have a chance of bettering these goals. We might say to a player, "We want at least 15 points a game from you and a 50 percent shooting average." To another player we will insist he make 45 percent of his shots and 10 points a game. Maybe these figures are way off for some coaches, but we feel that the lowest percentage we can allow the shooters is a 40 percent figure. Anything less than that is a result of not using the proper techniques, selection of shots, or not taking the shots from the high percentage areas.

We give the players a formula for shooting. We take their projected shooting percentages and the percentage spots on the floor, add them together, and divide by two. This equals the player's chance of scoring.

EXAMPLE OF A SHOOTING FORMULA

	Player Field Goal Perc.		Percentage Spot on Floor			Chance of Scoring
Player #1	(50%	+	50%)	÷ 2	=	50%
Player #1	(50%	+	70%)	÷ 2	=	60%
Player #2	(40%	+	40%)	÷ 2	=	40%
Player #2	(40%	+	70%)	÷ 2	=	55%
Player #3	(35%	+	40%)	÷ 2	=	37½%
Player #3	(35%	+	70%)	÷ 2	=	52½%

It doesn't take long after the season starts for the players to be convinced that the statistics are accurate. Now we have the players motivated to take good shots at good percentage positions on the floor.

We also set goals for the rebounders. They are always conscious of their rebounding average. In all my years of coaching I haven't had a player who didn't want to better that average. This is one of the categories that we don't mind a player setting a record in as long as he is rebounding within the "Big Three" concept.

When we post the statistics sheets, we mark arrows pointing up or down at each average indicating an improvement or decline in the statistical performance of each player since the last game. Thus, the stats become a matter of pride and thus a source of motivation.

The Last-Pass

The last-pass statistic is the most controversial one we have. Can you imagine the look on a coach's face when he tells us his point guard has a 6.3 assists per game and we say, "That's fine, but our forward has a 7.2 last-pass average"?

As we explained in Chapter 1, assists are included in the last-pass average, but they are not singled out. The guard that has the 6.3 assist average is singled out for helping his teammates score nearly 13 points per game. Our forward gets the ball into the hands of players who score over 14 points a game. Which statistic is more impressive?

We realize that the guard has some last passes he should get credit for, but who knows whether he has them or not? However, we would know. What it does for us is build a pride in each player that he is moving the ball and helping in the point production of his teammates. Players receiving assists give a "thank you" gesture to a teammate who helps him in getting the basket. Our team feels the same gratitude for getting the last-pass.

In most offenses, the guards or point guard has the most assists because they handle the ball the majority of the time. With the last-pass, any player on the floor can be the leader.

A good last-pass statistic in a game is approximately one-sixth of the team's number of field goals.

When we began recording the last-pass, our passing improved considerably. The passes are not only sharper, but the ball is moving better to the scoring areas. Its biggest asset is the players' feeling of helping each other out in the offensive scoring.

SUMMARY

There are a lot of books and articles written on statistics. There are probably even a greater number of such writings on shooting, rebounding, and passing. We decided to include these in this book to emphasize the need for every coach to define what he means by fundamentals.

We believe if you expect a lot from athletes, they will usually live up to your expectations. We also believe that they should be forced to work hard so they can live up to their capabilities. We believe in hard work and we *insist* that the players carry out the fundamentals necessary to play good basketball and to execute the Pick-and-Screen offense.

After we use the insistent coaching method and a player is still not carrying out the proper fundamentals, then we have to find other ways to get his attention. We are very fortunate to have an older gym. There happens to be a stairway leading up to the balcony. When the shooting gets sloppy, we have the players run the stairs. Every player knows that there are exactly 18 steps to the top. The players also know that if they take a poor shot they will run the stairway 100 times. We are lenient, however—if they make the shot, then they only run it 50 times. This stairway has become a tradition with our teams over the years. A funny thing about the stairway: you won't see any veterans running it—just the first-year men.

The secret in developing the guards as quarterbacks of the offense is making them understand their own strengths and limitations and also those of their teammates. We are firm believers in not putting anyone in a situation in which he cannot perform to his maximum.

We realize that the best motivation of them all is the *bench*. If a player is not doing the job, the bench can become a method of motivation. However, by setting individual statistical goals, the players work harder in drills, thus improving their fundamental skills. The next chapter will illustrate the offensive drills that help us in executing the Pick-and-Screen offense.

11

DRILLS TO MAKE
THE PICK-AND-SCREEN WORK

THEORY OF DRILLS

We do not believe in having drills just for the sake of drills. Each drill should have a definite value in helping the players carry out the coach's definition of fundamentals. The drills should also be of such variety that they complement the offense. We also like drills that not only create a relaxed atmosphere, but also include the basic fundamentals and will also develop individual and team competitiveness.

We experiment now and then with new drills, but we always seem to come back to the drills illustrated in this chapter. We do not hesitate to discard a drill after evaluating it over a short period of time. The first drill we ever discarded was the old standby three-man weave. In this drill one player passes to another player and runs behind him until the last player receiving a pass shoots a lay-up.

We analyzed this drill and noticed a lot of traveling taking place. Secondly, not many offenses have three men weaving down the court. This is one drill that goes against good fundamentals and it does not complement any particular offense.

Snap Shoot

The first thing we do at the start of every practice is snap shoot. This means that two players work together. One player has the ball and is three feet from the basket while the other player rebounds. The shooter puts the ball over his head in a "C" position and takes a shot. We want a full extension of the arm and the hand snapping into the basket. We want the player to get used to putting the ball in the basket. We emphasize the snap so there will be a back spin on the ball. After ten shots the shooter becomes the rebounder. Each day the players move around so they shoot from a different angle. As the season goes on, we will back up farther away from the basket, but never more than thirteen feet.

A player is never allowed to shoot a ball until he has done his stretching exercises. These are all done before practice starts along with some ball-handling drills that are so popular with most teams. We make sure that when practice starts the players are ready for the snap shooting drill.

One-Step Lay-ups

We try to work in pairs as much as we can. We also use every basket in the gym. The player with the ball lines up on the free throw lane line just far enough away from the basket so that he is able to shoot a lay-up after taking only one step. After his lay-up, he rebounds the ball and passes to his partner, who then steps and shoots. The players are constantly reminded during the drill to "step-shoot, step-shoot." We convince the players that the most important part of a lay-up is the last step before the shot. There is no reason to waste time practicing lay-ups from near midcourt if you haven't mastered the one-step lay-up. After a certain number of shots, we will switch to the other side of the basket.

One-Dribble Lay-ups

Now the pair will move back so they can dribble, step, and shoot. After a certain number of shots, they move to the other side of the basket. No matter how far out on the court you practice lay-ups, the last dribble, step, and shot are the important factors of the lay-up. At times we make this competitive by using a 30-second time limit. The pair with the most lay-ups made in that amount of time is the winner.

Swing Shot

The two players line up for the one-dribble lay-up, but this time they head toward the baseline bringing the ball to one side (shoulder high) and then they swing their shooting arm toward the backboard. They hang on to the ball with two hands as long as possible while turning their hips toward the basket. This is the same technique as a hook shot. We encourage this shot in order to get the ball over a taller defensive man who is contesting the lay-up.

Cross-Over Shot

The two players are lined up for the one-dribble lay-up, but this time they use one dribble, cross over to the opposite side of the basket, and shoot a swing shot.

30-Second Shooting

Each pair lines up on the end of the free throw line and just inside the semicircle toward the basket. This is the 70-percent shooting area, so we want the players to build confidence in their shooting from that spot. One player shoots a jump shot, rebounds his own shot, and passes the ball to his partner. They continue this pattern for 30 seconds. They then move to the other side of the free throw line and repeat the shooting drill. The pair with the most total shots is the winner.

Short-Shot Drill (Diagrams 11-1 a,b,c)

In this drill we want to combine the lay-up with the jump shot. We divide the team into two groups, one at each end of the court. Each group has a leader who sets up each new move in the drill. After the players execute a move from one side of the basket, they move to the other side and repeat it from that side. Diagram 11-1a depicts the start of the drill. The leader

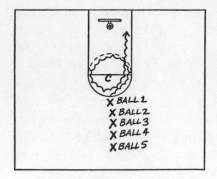

Diagram 11-1a

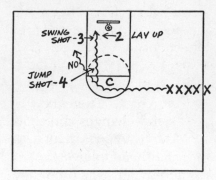

Diagram 11-1b

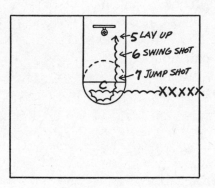

Diagram 11-1c

dribbles around the circle as fast as he can while straddling the line and ends up going in for the lay-up. As soon as the leader makes a full circle, the next player in line starts his dribble right behind the leader. We want the man shooting to stay inside the free throw lane as he makes his final move to the basket. This teaches the players to cut directly to the basket rather than rounding off their move, which would allow the defense to catch up with them.

Diagram 11-1b shows the second, third, and fourth parts of the drill. A coach stands on the center of the free throw line and checks to see if the players are protecting the ball and dribbling low when going by a defender. The coach should also keep reminding the players to execute each shot properly and to stay inside the free throw lane on their drive to the basket. In the third part of the drill the players cut for the basket, but this time they shoot a swing shot. In the fourth move the players pull up in the 70 percent area and shoot a jump shot.

Diagram 11-1c illustrates the fifth, sixth, and seventh parts of the drill. The player dribbles with his left hand until he is past the coach. Then the player pivots with his back to the basket and changes direction. He is now dribbling with his right hand and goes in for a lay-up. In the sixth part he shoots a swing shot and follows that with a jump shot in the 70 percent area to end the seventh and final part of the drill. Remember that we do every part of the drill on each side of the basket so that there are actually 14 moves to this drill.

Quick Shooting for Guards

The guards pair up and go to a basket. One guard shoots and the other rebounds. The rebounding guard backspins the ball off the floor away from the shooter but not more than 16 feet from the basket. The shooting guard quickly moves to that spot, catches the ball as it bounces up, and then takes a quick jump shot. This is repeated five times. The guards then exchange positions. Any number of repetitions can be used. We want the guards getting to the point of making at least four out of five shots. As the season progresses, the shots can be taken farther away from the basket. We want the guards to learn to shoot quickly but still maintain the proper techniques of shooting.

Deep-Man Combination Drill

Diagram 11-2 depicts the lineup for the drill. Both 2 and 5 have a ball. We alternate the drill from one side to the other. Player 2 first tries to feed 3 as he is posting on the big block on the free throw lane. Player 3 carries out all the posting techniques that were illustrated in Chapter 10. The defensive man X^3 must vary his defensive position on 3 by alternating between the high and low side and both behind and in front of the man posting. We use forwards as well as guards in the 2 and 5 positions. The feeders try to create passing angles by the use of a dribble or a pass. If 2 cannot get the ball into the post, he can pass the ball to 1, who will look to the post men. Player 1

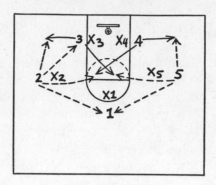

Diagram 11-2

can also pass back to 2, and 2 again tries to feed 3. When 3 gets the ball and shoots, then 5 is ready to feed 4. When we are satisfied with the moves of the post man, we then have the post men break toward the sidelines. When the post man receives the pass, he faces the defensive man and drives on him one-on-one to the basket or pulls up for a jump shot.

When we are satisfied with the corner moves, the deep men flash across to receive the pass in the free throw lane. Player 2 feeds 4 and alternately 5 passes to 3. Player 1 is always looking for a pass from 2 or 5 and either passes to the deep man or makes a return pass to either 2 or 5.

The guards who are not in the feeding positions are doing the quick shooting drill at the other basket. After a time, the guards who are feeders move to the other baskets to work on their quick shooting and the quick shooters become the feeders for the deep post men.

DRIBBLING

Half-Court Dribble Tag

There are a lot of dribbling drills, but there are only two that we like to use. One of them is the half-court tag drill. Two players are holding a ball; one will be "it," and the other will try to avoid the tag by the "it" player. If a player is tagged, he becomes "it."

The players must stay within the boundaries of the half court. If one player goes out of bounds or his ball does, he becomes "it." In the first round they will each dribble with their right hand and tag with their left hand. They have 30 seconds to avoid each other's tag. After 30 seconds the player who is "it" is the loser. He puts his ball down and runs a lap or does some finger tip push-ups. In the second round the players dribble with their left hand and tag with their right. In the third round they dribble and tag with either hand. Once the players know the rules of the drill, we add at least six more pairs to the game. Now there are six separate tag games going on within the boundaries of the half court at the same time. At the end of 30 seconds there will be six balls laid down on the floor and six players running a lap. Twelve new players now pair up for their first round. The number of players in the drill at one time is left up to the coach's discretion.

In this drill, the players must keep their heads up for obvious reasons. They will be dribbling in every direction possible to avoid the tag and they will get used to dribbling in a crowd. This simulates penetration or a fast break situation. We can't think of any other dribble drill that teaches so many different dribbling fundamentals and is still fun and competitive.

Circle Dribbling

This drill is used to teach the player to protect the ball with the off hand or with the player's body. It also reminds him to keep the ball low while in a crowd. Two or more players have a ball and line up with both feet within one of the circles at the free throw lane or at midcourt. We prefer to put no fewer than six players in the circle at one time in order to create more of a competitive attitude. On the start signal, the players must dribble the ball and try to knock the ball of each other player out of the circle. A player is eliminated once his ball goes outside of the circle and he cannot retrieve it by reaching outside of the circle and still keeping one foot in the circle.

This drill also instills an attitude in every player that he should go after every loose ball. When there are only two players left in the circle, the eliminated players will count out loud to 15. We only allow 15 seconds for one player to become the champion of that round. If after 15 counts there are still two players left, then there is no winner for that round. The time element speeds up the action and also keeps the other players from standing around too long.

It is up to a coach how many times he would like to repeat the drill and what reward the champion will receive.

The preceding dribbling drills are the only drills we designate as dribble drills. We feel that the players get enough dribbling practice with the short shot drill, fast break drills, or any other drill that includes the use of the dribble, including scrimmages and special situations.

PASSING
(Diagram 11-3)

Semicircle

In this drill we use two basketballs. Player 1 is holding one ball and 2 has the other. On the start signal 2 passes his ball to 1 as 1 is passing his ball to 3. Player 3 will then pass to 1 as 1 passes to 4. The passes continue clockwise or counterclockwise from one end of the semicircle to the other with each man in line getting a pass. We also run the drill by having other men in the row receive a pass. You will notice in the diagram that 2 and 6 are in a direct line with 1. This helps to improve the players' peripheral vision. We also run the drill by using nothing but bounce passes. We also have the players call out the name of the player they are passing to. This helps in the player communication that is so necessary in basketball.

We quickly change from one sequence to another by a coach's command. While the players are running the drill clockwise and passing the ball to every next man in line, a coach will give the command, "When I say change, I want you to rotate to your right, stagger pass counterclockwise, and call out each other's names—Ready, change." This part of the drill helps the players to *listen* to a coach's instructions. It really helps when you have to make adjustments during a game and the players have learned to listen to you.

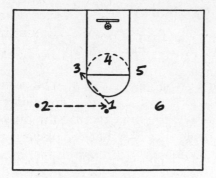

Diagram 11-3

Around the Circle (Diagram 11-4)

Players 1 and 2 shuffle around the circle clockwise as fast as they can while passing a ball back and forth using a two-handed chest pass. On the command, "Change," they move counterclockwise.

We incorporate this drill with the 30-second shooting drill so that players are not standing around waiting their turn. Part of the team will use the side baskets for the 30-second shooting drill and the others will use the three circles on the main floor for passing. We like this drill because it teaches the players to concentrate on passing to a moving target. This drill helps in getting the ball into a shooter's hands while he is breaking to a shooting area or when he is flashing through the free throw lane.

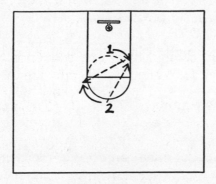

Diagram 11-4

Feed the Post (Diagram 11-5)

Two players stand on opposite sides of the free throw lane facing each other. A third player is in the lane and tries to stop the passes as they go from one man to the other. The players passing the ball are not allowed to feed the ball over the top or hold the ball over their heads. The third player must always come up on the man with the ball. If the ball is intercepted, then the player that passed the ball becomes the defensive man. This drill was designed to help the players in feeding the post man while maintaining a good threat position.

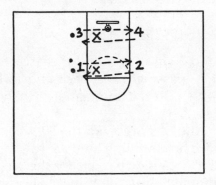

Diagram 11-5

Bad Pass Drill

The players pair up and line up on opposite sides of a free throw lane. One player has a ball and the other has his back turned to the ball. A coach stands at midcourt and gives the command, "Ball." The man with the ball passes the ball any-where but chest high. When the man with his back turned hears "Ball," he quickly turns and tries to catch the bad pass. Now the man who passed the ball will turn his back on the ball and wait for the command, "Ball."

This drill teaches a player to react quickly and do every-thing possible to catch every pass thrown to him. We let the players know that anyone can catch a good pass but it takes a good athlete to catch every pass.

REBOUNDING

Our offensive rebounding is always done five-on-five. Because of our offensive rebounding rules, we haven't found a drill that we could break down into one-on-one, two-on-two, etc. We feel that we get the best results when we work on rebounding when we run the Pick-and-Screen offense. This includes the fast break, working against man-to-man or zone presses, and special situations.

We are so intent on having good rebounding position that we are willing to stop practice any time there is someone out of position. The player out of position will let the coach know what rule he should have used to put him in the right position. Once the player understands his mistake, then we resume practice.

Form Rebounding

Players pair up and line up on opposite sides of the free throw lane. One player tosses the ball into the air toward the other player, using a two-handed underhand pass and making sure there is backspin on the ball. The rebounder uses the proper techniques and power jumps to rebound the ball. We want the rebounder to make a half-turn as he comes down with the ball. In this way the players get used to keeping their backs to the player they are rebounding against. The man tossing the ball up should vary the height of his toss and also the area in which the ball comes down. We want the rebounder to learn how to move under the ball before he goes up, instead of just reaching out for the ball.

FAST BREAK DRILLS

We don't believe there is such a thing as a four-on-three break or a five-on-four, so our drills never exceed the limit of three-on-two. We do include a trailer when we work as a full team; however, he seldom gets into the action of the break. We have that position covered, however, because it fits into our theory of never leaving anything to chance.

32-21 Fast Break

    Diagram 11-6 illustrates the lineup for the start of the drill. Player 2 faces the basket and throws the ball against the backboard. Player 2 rebounds the ball and uses 1 or 3 as his outlet pass. In the diagram, 2 passes to 3 and then cuts behind 3 to fill the outside lane. Player 3 dribbles into the middle lane to set up the three-on-two break. If the offense scores, or the defense steals the ball or rebounds a missed shot, the two defensive players then start their fast break. Player 3 took the ball down the middle on the initial break, so he has to hustle back and become the defender on the two-on-one break. When the two-on-one break is over, the next three players in line step out on

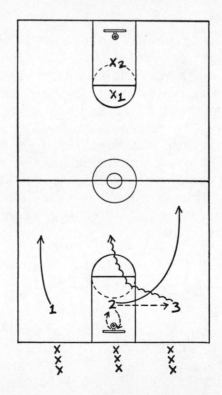

Diagram 11-6

the court and repeat the three-on-two break against 1 and 2, who stayed down at the other end of the court.

Scramble Break

We decided to use this fast break drill because we believe that it is a lot harder to clear the ball out of the back court on the break than it is to score at the other end. This is one drill that has really helped us in the transition game. It is an aggressive drill that helps the players clear the back court and teaches them to stay on the ball and not settle for just one shot on the fast break.

Diagram 11-7 illustrates the initial lineup for the start of the drill. A coach shoots the ball and then steps off the court. As soon as the offense takes one shot, the third man on defense steps out on the court and helps the other two defensive men.

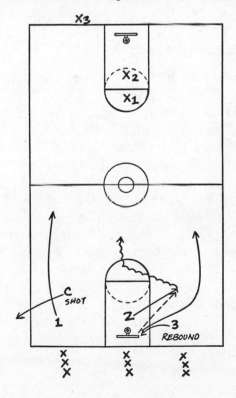

Diagram 11-7

As long as the offense keeps rebounding the ball, they are allowed to score. The defense must get possession of the ball, or the offense will keep putting the ball in the basket. There are no boundary lines in this drill while the players are scrambling for the ball. However, once the defense rebounds or steals the ball they have to start their fast break within the boundaries of the court.

When the defense starts its break, the original offensive team tries to stop it. They are allowed to do this up to the midcourt line. If they steal the ball before it gets to midcourt, they again try to score. If the defense gets the ball past midcourt line, they are now on a three-on-two break and are considered the offensive team. We usually set a time limit on the drill.

We also think up some nice things for the defense to do if they allow more than five baskets on a single break.

Quick Break—Baseball Pass

This drill was formulated to simulate the quick fast break that was illustrated in Chapter 9.

Diagram 11-8 depicts the lineup to start the quick break drill. On a start signal, 1 and 2 break for the opposite basket and look for a baseball pass from 7 and 8. When 1 and 2 catch the ball, they immediately pass to 4 and 3. Players 3 and 4 then pass back to 1 and 2 so they can shoot a lay-up. Players 3 and 4 rebound the ball, step out-of-bounds outside the free throw lane, and look to throw the baseball pass to 7 and 8 who are breaking to the opposite baskets. Players 5 and 6 now move into the free throw circle, looking for a pass from 7 and 8.

After 1 and 2 shoot, they keep moving to the rebounding lines. The rebounders stay in the shooting line after passing the ball to the breaking players. After a set time we say, "Switch," and all the players move to opposite sides of their respective positions on the court. Now the shooters will be shooting on the left side of the basket.

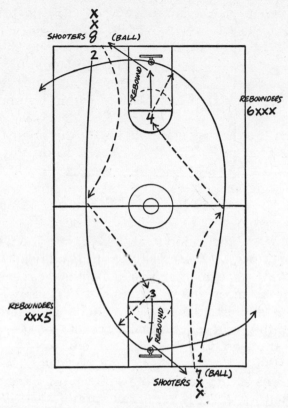

Diagram 11-8

TWO-ON-TWO DRILL

This drill is the heart of the offense. We run this drill every day. The drill is executed as the title says—two-on-two. We have the best guards going at each other with the best forwards and centers teamed up with them.

We use every possible basket in the gym by starting out on the right side of each basket. This is the Pick-and-Screen at its best.

In Diagram 11-9, G^1 has the ball and F^1 is practicing his screen-and-post techniques.

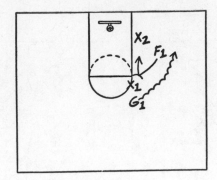

Diagram 11-9

If G^1 passes the ball to F^1 at the wing position, G^1 goes to the center to practice his move out of the corner.

We draw a line down the middle of the court and no one is allowed to score on the other side of that line. The reason behind this is to simulate back-side help. There are six other players on the court in a normal game situation, so you don't get many shots on the other side of the basket.

This drill also give a chance for each player to work on his tough screens, clean picks, and his power dribbling and shooting. Insistent coaching is very important in the drill. We want the players to pick and screen at their best. We first work the right side of the basket and then switch to the left.

The main rule of the drill is that if you pass to a player, screen for him, and roll and post, the man with the ball must look to shoot and then to pass.

RELAY RACES

Diagram 11-10a depicts the lineup for the shooting segment of the relays. Two teams are lined up approximately 14 feet to the side of the basket and the other two teams in the 70 percent shooting area. On a start signal, the player with the ball in front of each line shoots the ball. He rebounds his own shot and passes to the next player in line. This relay continues until one of the teams makes 10 baskets. That team is the winner of the

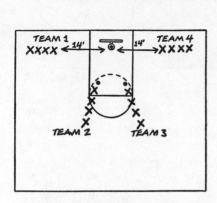

Diagram 11-10a

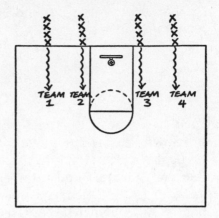

Diagram 11-10b

first round and receives three points for its effort. The other three teams continue until second place (2 points) and third place (1 point) are determined. When all the teams are finished, we rotate clockwise and start again. We usually rotate once and then go into the dribble segment of the relays. Each team lines up as indicated in Diagram 11-10b. Each player in front of the line has a ball in his hands. On a start signal, the players with the ball dribble the length of the court with their strong hand and shoot a lay-up. Once they score at the other end, they must rebound their own shot and dribble back and score at the basket near the starting position. They then pass the ball to the next man on their team. After the second man receives the pass behind the baseline, he dribbles to the other end with his strong hand to score. When everyone on a team has gone through the complete relay ahead of the other teams, that team is the winner. Teams are again scored three, two, and one point as they finish from first through third.

In the second round, the players dribble and shoot with their weak hand.

We like to incorporate this drill into the shooting drill. We finish one round of shooting and then rotate clockwise. We then run the relay races the length of the court with the strong and weak hand. We then finish the drill with the last two rounds of shooting and then add up the total scores. We then have some nice things for the winners and not-so-nice things for the non-winners, depending upon where they finish in the relay races.

SUMMARY

Each one of the drills is very important to the offense. For some unknown reason our players always get excited about these particular drills. It is one reason why we use them. I believe there are an unlimited number of drills that can result in the same degree of accomplishment of fundamental techniques, but the drills that are accepted by the coaches and players alike are the most rewarding. When I attend clinics and get excited about certain drills, I try them on our players; if they get excited, I get excited.

All the drills mentioned in this chapter have been accepted by the coaches and, more importantly, by the players.

12

BLENDING PICK-AND-SCREEN INTO ANY SYSTEM

It was a lot of fun putting this offense together. We realize that not many coaches will adopt it entirely. We do believe, however, that parts of this offense can be blended into any offense.

We are extremely proud of the fact that other coaches have acknowledged their respect for the discipline so evident in the Pick-and-Screen offense.

In the preceding chapters the blending of the Pick-and-Screen into a variety of sets was illustrated. We know from experience that any style of offense can benefit by the use of tough screens and picks.

There are only so many successful plays in basketball and there are only so many sets. It is the combination of these which make a coach's offense unique.

When I became the varsity coach at Cretin High School I had not settled on what offense I was going to use. When I was the sophomore coach I experimented with different alignments such as a 1-4 and a 3-2 set. It was in my first varsity season I started to piece together the Pick-and-Screen offense.

I started with a two-guard offense because my assistant coaches agreed that the two-guard front would be more feasible with the personnel we had.

At that time we didn't have any good ball-handling guards. We had to find a way to help the guards offset their deficiencies in ball handling but still make use of their talents. By using a two-guard offense we had the guards playing on the free throw boundary line extended. This allowed them to make a shorter pass to the forward with a better passing angle.

We also felt that the guard without the ball could get back to the half-court line in a hurry if he saw the ball being stolen by the defensive guard or intercepted by a defensive forward on the initial pass. In other words, we always had one guard covering for the other.

When we evaluated the offense after the first season, our first surprise was the way the guards had competed all season and never once did the guards' ball handling hurt the execution of our offense.

As each of the following seasons ended with more success than the preceding one, we naturally stayed with two guards and have continued it to this day. Even when we run the 3-2 set as shown in Chapter 5, we have two guards in the game, one of them lining up in a wing position.

The 3-2 set is our version of a 1-4 set and the popular 1-2-2. We have also experimented with a shuffle offense and the 1-3-1 alignment.

With the 1-3-1 set or any other point-guard offense, we found that we could run the guard special, double screen in the corner, and some part plays from the high post. All we had to do for the high post was to have the point guard pass to the wing and cut by in front of the center (middle of free throw line) away from the ball. The wing away from the ball would then break across in front of the center and break toward the basket, completing the high post scissor as shown in Diagram 12-1. The double screen for the forward can also be used as illustrated in Diagram 12-2.

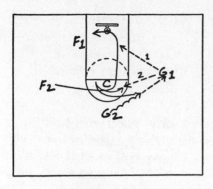

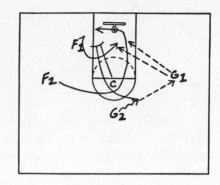

Diagram 12-1   **Diagram 12-2**

Chapter 5 shows how the low post plays can be blended into the 3-2 set, which is comparable to the 1-4 and 1-2-2 sets.

We know from these experiments that part plays from the Pick-and-Screen can be blended into any set.

However, part plays were not what *we* wanted. We wanted the whole package. With a two-guard offense, we found it easier to coordinate the entire Pick-and-Screen offense into a synchronized movement.

We believe that two particular seasons are worth mentioning at this time. After five successful years with the system we finally had a season where we were really struggling offensively. We confess that we started to doubt the offense and did what a lot of coaches do—we asked for help from other successful coaches. We thank those coaches for their concern and their honesty in presenting their systems to us. We were really excited when they first presented their ideas to us. We felt we were now ready for our new surge on the basketball world. About 15 minutes before the next practice, we abandoned the whole idea and decided to stick with what we knew best—the Pick-and-Screen. We are glad we did, because that was the first year Cretin High School won a state championship in 18 years.

Three years later we started the season with two straight losses and the offense was pathetic. Again we approached another successful coach and asked for his help. Again, we abandoned the idea at the last minute and ended up with another state championship.

Since those two early incidents, we have never doubted what we are trying to do. We have learned the meaning of patience and hard work.

Now we are getting requests from other coaches to help them take parts of the Pick-and-Screen offense and work those parts into their styles of play.

One coach who contacted us was using what he called a "passing" game. He didn't want to change his style entirely because he had had success with it and he had confidence in it. What he was looking for was some way to free a forward who was an excellent shooter but could not go one-on-one.

We told him about the deep twin screen that we use with the high post set and the forward special play. The most important help we gave him was to show him how certain passes, if added to his system, could trigger the double screen. The forward special was much easier because the coach always had his guard pass and screen away. With the forward special the guard would pass to the forward and go over to the forward to get the ball.

Another coach was using a shuffle and wanted to blend in the peek series. We not only worked the peek into his offense, but we showed him a way that he could use the series and still bring his shuffle back to the original set.

The reason we mention these experiences is to point out that any team can use parts of this offense to shore up its offensive attack.

We firmly believe that once you cross midcourt with the ball, you are now on the offensive attack. The way you get to this position we consider full-court strategy. We have always looked for ways to get the ball into the front court as soon as possible. This is one of the phases of the game in which we do best. We have been pressed from day one since we started using the Pick-and-Screen offense. Yet to this day, we cannot recall a time when we lost a game as a result of a press. The few simple moves we use against man-to-man or zone presses have been very effective.

We realize that there is more to an offense than just working against a soft, half-court, man-to-man offense.

We do, however, believe that the key to the half-court, man-to-man attack is the variety of screens we use. We are not always using the same type of screen, so the defense has a tough time making adjustments.

We know that teams which use the screen in their attack would be more effective if they used more than just a belly-up screen.

What adds to our offensive effectiveness is the use of the back-on screen and the tandem screen, along with the twin screen.

The key to using screens away from the ball is to camouflage them. We accomplish this by using a back-on screen. A belly-up screen away from the ball alerts the defense to the fact that they are being screened and as a result they can adjust or switch on the play. However, with the back-on screen the defensive players don't realize that they are being *used* and cannot help each other.

The tandem screen is effective because not many offenses use it. Therefore, not many teams practice against it and their players are not used to fighting through one screen right after another.

Coaches who like to use the screen-and-roll can substitute the roll for the screen-and-post as discussed in this book. We gave the reasons for not using the roll. The most important reason was that it was not effective against the new defenses now in use. In order for the roll to be effective, a team has to spend a lot of time practicing it. We didn't want the screener to become the number one man in the Pick-and-Screen offense. What we wanted from the screener was a tough screen to free the man with the ball to shoot a good percentage shot.

We don't want the screener to worry about the defensive man going over the top or behind his screen.

We don't want to take up a lot of our practice time teaching the screener to recognize these defensive moves. The screener would also have to learn the proper footwork on his pivots in order to keep the defensive man on his back when he rolls to the basket. With the screen and post we don't have to teach any special rolls to get to the post position.

We mentioned previously that we use a considerable variety of screens and we use them in equal amounts during a game. Therefore, it would not be to our advantage to spend extra time trying to perfect just one of the screens.

Furthermore, the majority of the screens are predetermined, so the man doing the picking has the responsibility of maneuvering his defensive man into the screens.

We have also been called an "upset-minded team" by the sports writers. A coach asked us one time, "If you are such a great upset team, why don't you win all your games?" Our reply was, "If we were upsetting every team we played, there would be no upsets." We believe that the experienced coach knows what we are trying to say, and the inexperienced coaches will someday glory in the feeling of beating a team rated a heavy favorite over his team.

We are very excited about the Pick-and-Screen offense along with the pressure and zone offenses. There are a lot of great coaches and teams that we must work against, so we have to be well-prepared. When we combine the offense with the out-of-bounds plays, we are ready for a winning season.

We have mentioned in an earlier chapter that the better the player, the better the results with this offense. We keep mentioning this because we have done so well with players who, after graduating, never played beyond the Division III level in college.

We read so many tributes to the abilities of players in which coaches tell how many high school All-Americans or major college players they have coached, and how many of their players have gone into the professional ranks. It really excites us to think that our offensive strategies have survived without those highly publicized players. However, we wouldn't have traded any one of our players over the years because they were excellent young men who played to win. What more can a coach ask for?

When we play against or watch an outstanding individual player, we always wonder how much more effective that player would have been if he played in a system that would not only make use of his free-lance abilities, but would consistently free him for some easy baskets.

All the situations we talked about and illustrated in this book have worked for us for all these years and are very adaptable to other systems. I believe that the key to our personal success is the fact that we never have to change anything when we start a new season. I haven't had the luxury of being a 12-month basketball coach. Like the majority of coaches on the high school level, I have to teach a full load while helping out in two other sports. Also, the majority of our players play two or more sports. One of the sports is baseball, which they continue to play throughout the summer. Over the years we had a lot of basketball-baseball combination athletes drafted by professional baseball teams.

We believe that by using the Pick-and-Screen offenses we have compensated for all those interruptions. The returning players never have to learn anything new. All they have to do is polish the offense.

The greatest compliment a coach can receive is from his peers—the coaches he coaches against and the coaches who watch his teams play. We want to thank all the coaches who over the years gave our teams these fine compliments. We sometimes wonder how much more knowledge every coach would have if all coaches had the opportunity to present their ideas as we were fortunate enough to do in this book.

Although we have been at it for so many years, there is still so much to learn.

INDEX